PHILADELPHIA'S

BEST DIVE BARS

PHILADELPHIA'S BEST DIVE BARS

Drinking and Diving in the City of Brotherly Love

BRIAN MCMANUS

Brooklyn, New York

Printed in the USA
10 9 8 7 6 5 4 3 2 1

Gamble Guides is an imprint of
Ig Publishing
392 Clinton Avenue
Brooklyn, NY 11238
www.igpub.com

Author photo by Michael Persico

ISBN: 978-1-935439-20-2

To my gorgeous, hysterical and intelligent wife Jaime. You are my best foot forward, and you've got the world's most amazing rack.

ACKNOWLEDGEMENTS

A book like this couldn't be done without the suggestions of places from friends. It also couldn't be done without their accompaniment on many a long night and slow crawl across the city to unearth these gems. Thanks to all who did either: Alec Meltzer, Dan McQuade, Adamma Ince, Ryan Kattner, Brian and Alison Langner, Michael Persico, Richie Charles, Gabe and Zach Gliwa and anyone else who suggested a place I wouldn't have heard of otherwise or ventured out with me into the dark corners of neighborhoods we thought we knew pretty well, but found we didn't. Thanks also to Michael Alan Goldberg, who took all the pictures for the book and who generally makes work at my day job tolerable due to the quality and volume of hours he puts in. Without him, this book wouldn't have gotten finished. To that point, most of all I'd like to thank the esteemed Dr. Doug Osman, whose alcohol intake and easy nature with completely faced strangers left me in quiet awe over and over again during this project. You, sir, are a saint. Saint Arnold, patron saint of beer, to be exact.

Philadelphia's Best Dive Bars
(arranged by location)

CENTER CITY
12th Air Command
Bob and Barbara's
Bonner's Irish Pub
Cherry Street Tavern
CoCo's
Dirty Frank's
Doobie's
Las Vegas Lounge
Locust Bar
Locust Rendezvous
McGillin's Olde Ale House
McGlinchey's
Medusa Lounge
Midtown II
Oscar's Tavern
Paddy's Old City Pub
Pen & Pencil
Raven Lounge
Society Hill Hotel
Tattooed Mom
Tritone
Westbury Bar

SOUTH PHILLY
1201 Bar
12 Steps Down
Big Charlie's Saloon
Bonnie's Capistrano
Brother's Two
Burg's Lounge

Cookie's Tavern
DiNic's Tavern
The Dive
Dolphin Tavern
Fireside Tavern
Friendly Lounge
Grumpy's Tavern
Nickel's Tavern
Penns Port Pub
Ray's Happy Birthday Bar
Rosewood Bar
Triangle Tavern

NORTH PHILLY
Atlantis (The Lost Bar)
Billy's Chili Pot
Chug A Mug
Club Ozz
El Bar
El Cantinflas Bar & Taco Place
Era
Fishtown's 15th Round
Fishtown Tavern
Gil's Goodtime Tavern
Half Time Good Time
Jack's Famous Bar
Jerry's Bar
J.R.'s Saloon
Krupa's Tavern
Les-N-Doreen's Happy Tap

Little Station
Luke's Bar
Melrose Bar
Old Philadelphia Bar
OMAC's Place
R.U.B.A. Hall
Side Street Café
Tailgator's Sports Bar
Tony's Way
Westy's
Yesterday's Tavern

WEST PHILLY
Abby's Desert Lounge
Billie's Boomer Lounge
BJ Lounge
Blue Nile Falls
Caprice Villa Lounge
Cheers
Cousin Danny's Exotic Haven
El Toro
Fiume
Hide-A-Way Inn
Melody Lounge
New 3rd World Lounge
New Angle Lounge
Parkside Inn
Queen of Sheba
Smitty's Millcreek Tavern
Way's Lounge

MANAYUNK/ROXBOROUGH/ OFF THE BEATEN PATH
Cresson Inn
DeLeo's Café
Five Points Cocktail Lounge
Peck Miller's Bar
Pop Pop's II

GREAT NORTHEAST
Beef Seekers Inn
City Line Bar & Horseshoe Pits
Leneghan's Crusader Inn
Morrell Tavern
SmokeEater's Pub
Tailhook Tavern

Way's Lounge

Introduction

The laws governing the sale of alcohol in Pennsylvania are a hold-over from a time past, written in 1933 just after Prohibition ended. They're paternalistic. They're puritanical. But mostly, they're just plain ridiculous.

When I moved to this city from Texas a lifetime ago, I remember walking into a gas station to pick up a six pack of whatever was cheap. I asked the cashier where the beer was and he looked at me like I'd just told him I thought bestiality gets a bad rap. The state doesn't allow beer sales in gas stations, he told me. So I went to the grocery store, and found out that the state doesn't allow the sale of beer there either. Where the hell did I just move to, I wondered?

I eventually found out that beer in Philly is sold at some delis, bars with takeout licenses, and beer distributors, which only sell by the case. That's it. Liquor's worse, as it's only sold in stores run by the state. As a result, Pennsylvania has fewer liquor stores per person than any other state in the nation. And it's going backward—there are fewer liquor stores in the state today than there were in 2006. The liquor laws in Pennsylvania are so bad, people in Philly frequently drive to nearby New Jersey and Delaware to buy booze, an offense for which, if caught, they could spend up to ninety days in jail for committing. Seriously.

If there is a silver lining to be found in these ass-backward laws, it's what they've done to foster the bar culture here. Simply put, bars in Philly are ubiquitous, and because the state makes it as difficult as possible to buy hooch elsewhere, said bars are often packed. Happy Hour isn't just an idea here, it's a lifestyle. In Philadelphia, our time is divided into thirds—work, home, bar. We spend a lot of hours in our booze soaked halls, whether we're meeting friends, watching the Phillies, sipping suds in solitude, celebrating or grieving. And because Philly is such a walkable city, we often don't leave our bars until we're nice and soused. There's no wheel to get behind, so sure, I'll have another. Or ten.

The bars contained in this book are the city's most colorful, character-filled dives. But what exactly makes a bar a dive? To me, dive bars are like pornography: hard to define, but you know one when you see it. And, while one person's dive may be another person's upscale establishment, there are a few basic characteristics that define a dive. The smell of stale air. A few hardscrabble regulars. Low lighting. Red light bulbs. Ripped and warn leather booths or barstools. Wood walls. Faux-wood walls. Photos of regulars past and present stapled to those walls. Nicotine-caked ceilings. Surly service. A vague sense someone might do you bodily harm. Cheap, stiff drinks. Jukeboxes oozing music to help mend a broken heart or break it all the more. And, the piéce de résistance, something odd, out of place or downright illegal—be it a dog sitting on a barstool, a baby on the bar, an old man playing tonsil hockey with a tranny in a booth, or a drunk sobbing loudly to no one but himself. In short, the type of shit that would get you kicked outta someplace proper. Places that, if the owner dared raise the prices a nickel, he would hear a dimes worth of grief from his customers. Some of the bars in this book possess all these qualities, while others possess only a few. The rating system will help you navigate which places offer a simple fun night out, and which offer your possible last night on earth. Use it wisely.

Finally, the word "dive" isn't meant as a pejorative. Some bar owners might be insulted by it being used to describe their place, and for that I offer my sincere apologies. The intention here isn't to offend, but instead to shine a light on what I feel are some of the most unique and storied bars in our fine city, institutions of old, or in the making. I loved meeting some of the longtime owners of these places and saddling up bar side with many of their colorful regulars. I got mighty drunk in some of these establishments, and enjoyed them all very much (the exception being DeLeo's Café, which truly is a shithole). Though my liver is happy I'm done spending long hours, day in, day out, at these establishments, the rest of me is kinda bummed. It's been as fun as it's been physically crippling.

Rating System

One toothless old man at the bar.

One toothless old man under the bar.

One toothless old man behind the bar.

Leave your valuables at home.

Drink and be merry, for tonight you shall die.

A note about smoking

In 2007, Philly finally passed a smoking ban, which many major cities around the country had done years before. Only ours had an exemption: If a bar could show that less than 20 percent of its revenue was derived from food sales, smoking could continue in the bar. Thus, more of the bars in this book are exempt from the smoking ban than aren't. When that's the case, I make note of it in the blurb, more often than not with the phrase "smoke choked." (Hey, I tried.) For a list of all bars exempted by the smoking ban, simply Google the phrase "Philadelphia smoking bars," and a neat map *Philadelphia Magazine* did will pop up, though some of the places listed are veteran halls you most likely can't get into. Additionally, some of the smoking bars in this book aren't on that list, so it's not definitive. This book and that list used in tandem should do the trick should you be in the throes of a nic fit and in need of a bar that will accommodate.

Bob & Barbara's

CENTER CITY

12th Air Command

254 S. 12th St.
Phone: 215-545-8088

Dive Bar Rating

🍾🍾🍾

In the back of the front room of the cavernous first floor of gay dive 12th Air Command is a majestic painting of two noble, bucking white stallions. Smoke pours from their nostrils. Their manes float from their necks like drifting clouds. They look as though they're dancing. Their muscles are intricately painted with loving detail. In a framed poster on an adjacent wall is another horse, of sorts. Posing for Hollywood photographer Keith Munyan, this muscle man is dressed in camouflage pants. Above the waist, nothing but dog tags, his bulging pectorals and rippled abs glisten in the sunlight. He pours a canteen of water over his chest.

Despite rumors to the contrary, 12th Air Command is not straight unfriendly. (Although the hairy paintbrush attached to the key to the women's restroom may make you think otherwise.) They will gladly slide you a beer over the blue glass topped bar, even if it does seem as though it's taken them extra long to notice you. But the truth of the matter is, you wouldn't notice you at 12th Air Command either, because 1) You look nothing like the men in Keith Munyan photos or any of the subjects of the uber-erotic Ross Watson photos also hanging around the joint; and 2) Even if you do (but you don't), you are simply *not as fabulous as anyone here.*

Just look around. A throng of young black males with Mohawks, high heels and purses gather in cliques while sipping frilly drinks. That's right: *high heels and purses.* They all move together like a school of fab fish to the back room for what is easily the most entertaining karaoke in the city. Hosted by a flamboyant Asian named Tinh, you can choose songs in fifteen different languages, though one seems to be just fine. Tinh is happy to reward balls-out (not literally) performances by handing out cowbells, tambourines and wood blocks to help stoke the crowd that gathers at the stage. The second, fast half of Tina Turner's "Proud Mary," inevitably performed by one of the black queens in heels, will rip back your skull and take a shit in your mind. The lone, drunken white guy who is not me, gets up to sing Offspring's "Pretty Fly (For A White Guy)" to wild applause. I do a mediocre version of "Purple Rain," dedicating it to the stallions. Not the ones in the painting, but the ones here in the room, singing along.

Bob & Barbara's

1509 South St.,
Phone: 215-545-4511

You'd be hard pressed to find more Pabst Blue Ribbon memorabilia gathered in one place than at Bob & Barbara's, whose walls and shelves act as an unofficial PBR museum. The old PBR ads, posters, bottles, cans and the like are an interesting snapshot of the brand before its hijacking, preserving a time when a can of the brew was more working class reward than hipster standby.

Wrapped around a rounded bar encased with a red leather cushion to soften a harsh edge, B&B isn't just a PBR art gallery. It serves the actual stuff too, and lots of it. Order it with a shot of Jim Beam and you've just had what's known as the "citywide" special, which B&B's introduced to Philly just over a decade ago. Now, in most spots worth their salt in town, a shot of Beam and Pabst truly can be purchased as "a special" at varying price points, none lower than at Bob & Barbara's, where it'll cost you a measly three bones. But fair warning: just call it "a special" and not a "citywide" when ordering. For reasons unclear, the latter invokes the ire of some B&B bartenders, who run the gamut from overwhelmingly friendly to ice-cold nasty.

On top of its dirt-cheap specials, Bob & Barbara's has lots of extracurricular activities on various nights: you might catch a drag show, a drunken spelling bee, a theater troupe known as Dumpsta Playas, filthy standup comedy or one of the best freewheelin' jazz shows in town, The Crowd Pleasers (RIP Nate Wiley). On weekends, B&B's gets packed, and you'll be hard pressed to find a seat at the bar. The right half of the room has a few scattered tables, but is mostly standing room only. This, combined with whatever show is going on or music pumping loudly out of the jukebox, makes for less-than-ideal conditions if you're looking for a place to have a few (dozen) quiet drinks. The crowds on weekends may make it difficult to peep at all the PB-aRt on the walls too, so if you plan on doing so, I suggest grabbing a stool early in the day when the clientele is made up of more interesting hard-drinking lifers.

Bonner's Irish Pub

120 S. 23rd St.
Phone: 215-567-5748

The exterior of Bonner's suggests that it's not going to be anything more than your typical Irish pub. It's got the requisite shamrocks painted everywhere, with Kelly green doors breaking up the white walls. Pretty standard.

Inside, however, *Twilight Zone* weirdness abounds. Your bartender, instead of asking what you'd like to drink, may ask whether your nipples are brown or pink. Typically this is followed by the ten or so toothless, wrinkled men around the bar placing bets about said color of said nipples. It seems like an easy enough bet—if you're white, they're most likely pink, if you're black, they're probably brown. But then the bartender, a white woman, will show you hers. And lo, they are brown. A couple of the toothless men will then attempt, as best they can, to explain the science or genetics of it. "Blah, blah you're tan." "Blah, blah Italian." Another will stare way too intensely, long after the brown-nips-on-white-lady have said bye bye and retired to their cozy cotton home.

When not betting on nipples, the patrons of Bonner's are usually doing one of two things: drooling or talking about the Phillies or Eagles. There are a few rather large TVs at either side of the rather large bar, and during the season, little Phillies and Eagles schedules can be found on each of the tables. They're the only things in Bonner's that'll remind you you're re living in this decade. Though the place has only been around for about fifteen years, the building it's located in is as old as the men at its bar. Like them, it's also falling apart. The doors are off their hinges. The paint is peeling. The tile is chipped. The bathrooms at Bonner's are also from a century ago, back when people were as tiny as hobbits. You've seen bigger sinks in a dollhouse. Good luck finding toilet paper or paper towels. If you do, they'll likely be wet. There's no soap either.

Though never too busy, Bonner's is always choked with thick cigarette smoke, sometimes to the point where you can't see your fingers in front of your face. Or, for that matter, your nipples.

Cherry Street Tavern

22nd and Cherry
Phone: 215-561-5683

There are two counters at Cherry Street Tavern, the lush, historic 105-year-old bar that just so happens to host one of the city's most obnoxious softball teams (more on that in a sec). One of the counters is the bar, and behind it reasonably priced cocktails await, served with a smile. Behind the other counter stands a pleasantly plump man in an apron. He's the sandwich maker, and watching him work is a thing of beauty. That might be because, under the apron, he's wearing a shirt and tie, and that's just a classy look. Even if it's his first day on the job, it makes him looks like an artisan, someone who cares about the craft of constructing delicious stacks of high-gastronomy, cutting them in half, dipping them in jus, wrapping them in foil, and handing them to you, the eager customer. If you're eating in, he'll even slide down some horseradish or whatever else he thinks you might need. It's a wonderful thing, especially if you've already ordered a few stiff ones from counter one and are in desperate need of mopping up some of the damage being done to your stomach.

Much like the out-in-the-open sandwich maker in the shirt and tie, something about Cherry Street just feels like snapshot from a bygone era. The bar itself is sturdily constructed of rich, dark wood, and the back wall behind it is made of the same material, with gorgeously ornate etchings around the mirrors. At your feet is something that I've heard about existing in old bars countless times, but chalked up to myth—a trough running the length of the bar. When the place was a No Women Allowed Valhalla, men would piss where they sat, right into the tiled trough. You can still make out where the drains are.

The history and the look of the establishment, which was once owned by NFL legend John "Tex" Flannery, but sold to brothers Bill and Bob Loughery in 1990—can't be matched, but the things that bring the Cherry Street Tavern down a notch are the fact that whoever is in charge loves to blare KC & the Sunshine Band VERY FUCKING LOUDLY which will cause the Cherry Street Softball team to TALK FUCKING LOUDER STILL about the disappointing loss they just suffered at the hands of some other bar league team they should've trounced. I suggest coming during here during the off season.

CoCo's

112 S. 8th St.
Phone: 215-923-0123

Just one block from Independence Hall sits one of the largest diamond districts in the nation. At Philadelphia's Jeweler's Row—located on Sansom Street between Seventh and Eighth, and on Eighth St. between Walnut and Chestnut—there are literally hundreds of different jewelers, enough to make you believe that thousands of Philadelphians get engaged each and every day. Right in the middle of the jewels is a gem of a bar, Coco's, one of the only dives you'll probably ever go to that has a four course tasting menu.

The food at Coco's is a mixed bag (both in quality and choice)—top-notch burgers and sandwiches sit alongside attempts at old world haute cuisine specials of the day like trout amandine and Steak Delmonico. (The mussels and wings are popular). The service is sassy, and usually comes with a smile. And the drinks are cheap.

Owner John Cokos (spelled with a k, you'll notice) opened the place in 1984, and there's definitely a tinge of the '80s lofting mightily in the air, as not much has changed at Coco's in its twenty-seven years. It's still got its dingy carpet, the booths along the wall are a bit tattered, and the lighting is a bit drab. (The dark, wooden walls help with that). They've hung up a few large flat screen TVs, and CoCo's can be a good place to take in a game—big enough so as not to get cramped, its regulars mature enough to not get too rowdy.

Mike Callahan bought in about ten years ago to help Cokos out with the goings on, and the place attracts a younger clientele than it once did, though some seasoned vets remain. They sit together at the bar, eating crab quesadillas, kobe beef burgers and peanut butter and jelly sandwiches, and drinking cheap suds.

Dirty Frank's

13th & Pine Sts.
Phone: 215-732-5010

Smack dab in the middle of Philly's historic gayborhood, Dirty Frank's windowless, sign-less exterior is marked with classy murals featuring famous Franks. There's Frankenstein, soul singer Aretha Franklin, a hot dog, freak-rocker Frank Zappa, former Philadelphia mayor and noted hard-line racist Frank Rizzo, and Ol' Blue Eyes, crooner and noted hard-line racist Frank Sinatra. It's positively artsy—attractive even—and gives no clues as to the dive-y delights that await you inside.

Because where the outside of the place emphasizes the Frank, the inside emphasizes the Dirty. Or, as comedian and native Philadelphian Paul F. Tompkins once noted in an HBO comedy special, "Well, the official name of the bar was Frank's, but when you got in there you automatically added the 'dirty' all by yourself. The tables were dripping-wet with beer *all the time*." True. Frank's is dusty enough to give Miss Havisham pause, but it's oh so charming, with a diverse clientele, art from locals selling on the walls, dusty trinkets and odds and ends lining the shelves and even a modest library should you feel the urge to read at your soaking wet table.

The pitchers at Dirty Frank's appear to have never been washed, but most of the crud clinging to them is on the outside, so don't worry too much. If the prospect of pouring from a dirty vessel scares you, order the special instead. It wears the proud distinction of being Philadelphia's oddest, a kamikaze shot from a clear, unmarked bottle and a seven-ounce pony of Miller High Life or Rolling Rock, depending on what the bartender grabs.

The crowd is a diverse bunch made up of hipsters and the near-homeless, chatting amicably with gays from the neighborhood in the four-person booths that line the walls or the ratty barstools puking their cushions surrounding the square bar. Sing-along's to famous songs ("Sweet Caroline," etc) are all but required here, and fast friends are made without much effort. There's darts in the back underneath a storage area that looks perilously close to collapsing, and *Simpson's* pinball too. On weekends, the place is packed to the gills, and it can take quite awhile to get a weird special or dirty pitcher. Best to come on a weekday, but happy hours and late nights are often crowded too. No matter what time you visit, however, be sure to bring your own bottle of Pledge.

Doobie's

2201 Lombard St.
Phone: 215-546-0316

Dive Bar Rating

It's a few days after the world has learned that one of its brightest literary bulbs has dimmed forever. JD Salinger is dead! Inside Doobie's, an old man sits in a corner, mumbling. He's bearded, gray haired and missing a few teeth. On the TV behind the bar an old sci-fi movie is playing. "You know what I thought after I read *Catcher in the Rye*," the toothless guy says to no one in particular. "I thought, 'This Holden Caufield is a *huge pussy*.'" Another guy at the bar, enjoying one of Doobie's vegan menu items, takes the bait. Before you knew it, a third chimes in. Then a fourth. Then half the bar.

Drinkers at Doobie's, more than at other dives, seem to be up for discussion and debate. About intellectual matters, about being a pussy or otherwise. It's perhaps the only dive in Philly where you can watch an episode of *Jeopardy* with a roomful of drunks who know the answer to every question. Please don't mistake any of this—the Salinger talk, the sci-fi, the spirited intellectual—for pretentiousness, however, as putting on airs here will get you promptly dismissed.

Doobie's has a larger-than-most-dives collection of always-rotating craft beers. One night might see a variety of Dock Street brew or Fuller's. The chalkboard with the day's menu specials and weekly beer lists is constantly being updated, and all of the suds here—craft or no—can be had for relatively cheap. David Bowie, Iggy Pop and the like will keep you company from a stellar jukebox.

Compared to other center city dives, Doobie's is a different animal. Unlike Oscar's or Dirty Franks, Locust Bar or Bob & Barbara's, chances aren't great that you'll make new, fast friends here. It might be because the regulars are a tight knit crew, up for debating one another, but not someone they're unfamiliar with. It could be that, because it's so small, the close-talking with strangers is just uncomfortable, and therefore avoided. Or it could be because you're a *huge pussy*.

Las Vegas Lounge

704 Chestnut St.
Phone: 215-592-9533

Dive Bar Rating

Located across the street from two of the most upscale restaurants in the city, Chifa and Morimoto, the Las Vegas Lounge seems to have been opened by someone who took his love of the movie *Swingers* a bit too far.

The place positively revels in all things Sin City: pictures of the Rat Pack adorn blood-red walls, Elvis plays on the jukebox, and if you're here, chances are you're a big loser. (Hi-yo!) Unlike the city it's named after, there's nothing too glitzy about LVL. It's a tad run down, but spacious. The two pool tables in back usually aren't occupied. The late night crowd is made up primarily of cooks from across Chestnut who will, more than likely, talk about the shift they just finished. Listen closely and you might gain some insight on what it's like to cook for Iron Chefs Morimoto and Jose Garces, who own Morimoto and Chifa respectively. Or, better yet, order another 20-ounce Yuengling for $2.50. That's the Friday special, and it's the only time Las Vegas Lounge threatens to get too busy.

Much like Vegas proper, there's always a deal here, a buffet of sensory delights. Taco Tuesday's feature beef or bean tacos for $1, $2 bottles of High Life and not-terrible margaritas for $4. Philadelphia-brewed Yards gets some shine on Wednesdays, where you'll find 20-ounce drafts on tap for $4. While fried food is king, the burgers aren't half bad, and they serve a few different varieties: bacon bleu (which has bacon and bleu cheese), the smokehouse (it's smoked), four-cheese (features four cheeses), the South of the Border burger (packed with affordable prescription drugs) and something called a "veggie burger."

"You're so money and you don't even know it." So says Vince Vaughn in *Swingers*. That phrase happens to be on Las Vegas Lounge's website too. So long as we're quoting movies based in Vegas, here's this: "What happens in Vegas stays in Vegas. Except herpes. That shit'll come back with you."

Locust Bar

314 Main
Phone: 215-925-2191

Dive Bar Rating

Chances are you'll get drunk in Locust Bar. So drunk, in fact, you might leave your phone behind when you leave. The next day, you'll call youself from a friend's or very angry wife's phone and an old timer at the bar will answer. "Come on by," he'll say. You will offer him $20 for his trouble, but he will refuse. He will offer you a drink. You will accept. He will offer you another. You'll get up after a couple more, and shuffle to the door. "Hey," the old timer will call out, "You forgot your phone again!"

Referred to as both the "Low-Cost Bar" and the place where "real drinkers go," Locust is in truth a bit of both. Satisfying the former: they serve dirt-cheap wings, sloppy Joes for $4.25, roast beef dripping with jus for $5.50 and (on Wednesdays) pitchers of Yuengling for $5. (Other days of the week you'll pay $7.) The latter: just look at the bar, where old boys sit alongside regulars and other pruned and pickled barflies who might've given even the likes of Charles Bukowski pause.

Along a faux-wood paneled wall across from those old drinkers are a series of retro 1950s styled booths filled with a much younger set, mainly broke artist types whose fixed-gear bikes you'll find locked to anything sturdy out front. These kids can (and do) get rowdy, whether it be on a regular night or at Locust's famed Sunday karaoke, and sometimes the grizzled old timers at the bar do a lot of staring at them. The reverse is true too, and the place can occasionally look like it houses two different species looking at one another through glass at a zoo, studying one another intently. Listen closely enough and you can hear their thoughts. Old timers: "Did I ever act like that?" Young kids: "Will I ever look like that?" The answer to both, of course, is a resounding yes. But oftentimes the two species comingle, and make beautiful, twisted memories. Like the time I saw a young girl in skin tight gold lamé pants kiss a much older man with tongue after he gave her money for the jukebox. (His only request: "No rap.") Or the time a bartender poured a bunch of shots for whoever wanted them, just cuz.

One more thing: In a surly "Fuck you!" to the Jefferson Cancer Center across the street, smoking at Locust is allowed.

Locust Rendezvous

1415 Locust St.
Phone: 215-985-1163

Not to be confused with the Locust Bar a few blocks up, Locust Rendezvous (a tip: this one has the word "rendezvous" in its name) feels, at times, more like Atlantic City than Philadelphia. Here, you'll find some Olds playing trivia and discussing the performance they just took in at the Kimmel Center up the street.. And, after you've had enough of their specialty shots, chances are you'll hallucinate about a horse diving into a tiny pool of water. At the very least, come morning, your mouth will have a strange aftertaste akin to salt-water taffy.

Sometimes referred to as "The 'Vous," many of the waitresses, in fact, resemble a more hard-scrabbled Barbara Walters. They've been working here for a long time, and they know just how to treat you. They're always kind, and as efficient as can be when things start to get tightly packed, which is inevitable, as the mixed drinks are muscular, and the menu has something for everyone. You can choose burgers, grilled or fried chicken, broiled fish or all day omelettes as your stay-sober meal. None will disappoint. (Ok, the fish might disappoint.) Each night features a wild variety of drink specials: $2 bottles of Lionshead (always worth the puzzle caps) or shots of things you absolutely shouldn't have shots of, also for $2. Served in tiny plastic cups, said shots can range from bubblegum or root beer flavored vodka or something else that will give you the type of raging hangover that'll make you swear off alcohol forever.

Located just half a block from Avenue of the Arts, the crowd inside The 'Vous is as diverse as the shots and food it offers, with students from the University of the Arts mingling with older, well-to-do types who've stopped by unwittingly after the symphony. The overall physical interior is pretty nondescript, however, with gold railings hugging half walls, and real and fake plants giving the beige faux-wood walls a touch of color. There's always a long wait for the restroom, which is something to consider before you down another $2 bubblegum vodka shot. Because pink piss streaming down your pant leg or the back of your skirt is just not a good look.

McGillin's Olde Ale House

1310 Drury St.
Phone: 215-735-5562

Looking around McGillin's large hall of long, always-packed tables, it's easy to forget the incredible history of the bar. The beer has been flowing here since 1860—that's eleven years before the first brick was laid at City Hall. McGillin's celebrated its 150th anniversary in 2010, and is the oldest continuously operating bar in Philadelphia.

Originally named The Bell in Hand, the place got its current moniker from the workers who frequented the bar and called it McGillin's after the Irish immigrant, William McGillin, who owned the place and lived upstairs with, in what was no doubt a ringing endorsement of the rhythm method, his thirteen children. William died in 1901, and the bar was left to his wife, affectionately known as "Ma." She steered the ship through prohibition and kept command until her death at age 90 in 1937. The bar was then left to her daughter Mercedes, who in turn sold the place to her brothers, and in their family's hands it has stayed ever since. Old newspaper clippings about the bar cover the walls, and are worth taking the time to read before you give yourself an alcohol-fueled case of double vision.

The place is mammoth, and there's seldom a night where most every seat isn't filled. That's in part due to the wildly popular nightly specials, be they 35 cent jumbo wings, $6 Sirloin steaks, two tacos for a buck or $3 jumbo nachos. There's the dirt-cheap beer too, of course—$2 pints and $5 pitchers can be had most nights. On Wednesdays and Friday's, a popular karaoke DJ helps kick the energy into a higher gear. The patrons of McGillin's are on the younger side—college aged kids or young urban professionals fresh outta their cubicle—though a couple old heads remain. You'll catch them sitting at the bar, close to the taps, where they nurse their cheap beer in as much peace as the place can offer (not much). Upstairs is another large bar which is reserved for private parties, but is open to the public most weekends to accommodate the swelling crowds. When you're in there, you're standing in William's living room, so be a lady/gent and say hello to his ghost.

McGlinchey's

259 S. 15th St.
Phone: 215-735-1259

Dive Bar Rating

True story: a friend named Ryan, while out at Dirty Franks one night, borrowed some money from a notoriously rude and hard-drinking waitress who works the day shift at McGlinchey's. (It's rumored she has a PhD in Physics from Penn, but then cracked *Beautiful Mind* or *Shine* style after her head was filled with too much info.) He thanked her, and told her he'd gladly pay her back the next day. She told him to stop by McGlinchey's around noon, money in hand. He did. She was not there. He waited. And waited some more. After awhile the bartender asked if his name was Ryan. "Yes, it is." She threw him an apron. *Beautiful Mind* had called earlier in the day, and told her boss that Ryan would be covering her shift.

Stories like this are not uncommon at McGlinchey's, where odd seems to be commonplace and your waiter might not even have expected to be there. Every year for Valentine's Day, McGlinchey's offers a deal hopeless romantics can't refuse: two chilidogs, two bags of Herr's potato chips, and a tiny bottle of Cook's champagne for the low, low price of $9.88. It's like Cupid's wet dream. Never mind you'd have to be crazy to eat here, or that the Cook's is probably warm. It's the thought that counts.

Speaking of thoughts, the staff at McGlinchey's isn't usually thinking about you at all. The bartenders and waiters not named Ryan are mostly rude to such a degree you'll think they're putting you on. (Philly attytood, baby!) Exempted from the smoking ban, you can still light up here, and nearly everyone does. You'll leave smelling like an ashtray, with burning eyes to match. A faded photomural of a duck in a pond sits above a few warn out leather booths straight behind the entrance. To the right, a giant, square bar keeps you separated from bartenders who will try as long as they can not to acknowledge you. Once they do, your lager will come in a heavy, chilled mug that'll cost something that makes proper tipping harder than it has to be—$1.80 or $2.60, something like that.

Despite the rudeness, McGlinchey's is a Philly institution, and perhaps the only bar that already has its own book. Or, at the very least, its own book with an introduction by Jonathan Franzen. In 2005, photographer/McGlinchey's bartender Sarah Stolfa started taking pictures of the patrons that filled the barstools. The series of photos, "The Regulars," won her a student photography contest (she studied at Drexel) run by the *New York Times* which she later turned into said book. Stop by McGlinchey's to pick one up. Retail price is $22.95, or a five-hour wait shift.

CENTER CITY

PHILADELPHIA'S BEST DIVE BARS

Medusa Lounge

27 S. 21st St.
Phone: 215-557-1981

Dive Bar Rating

It's never not hot inside the Medusa. That could be because there are usually lots of people here, bumping, grinding, and dancing the night away, creating body heat so thick you can cut it with a knife. Medusa is a basement bar that hosts live music shows and DJs, and its clientele generally reflect this. They're young kids who aren't grossed out too easily (read: no problem using Medusa's notoriously awful restrooms.)

The place is the home of the $4 PBR and shot of whiskey, which is unheard of in this neighborhood, Rittenhouse, where old money sophisticates walk their perfectly quaffed poodles in the park and sip $15 dirty martinis at restaurants like Rouge, Parc and Barclay Prime, the latter of which sells a $100 kobe beef cheesesteak and $7,475 bottles of Château Cheval-Blanc, a French red that sells at retail for $399. You'll find none of that pinky-out shit at Medusa, where dance parties like Sex Dwarf (hosted by WXPN Kid's Corner producer Robert Drake), Boom Bap and We Snackin' keep the early adopters happy.

The space itself is dark, outfitted mainly in blacks and red. The walls are covered with flyers for upcoming events and an ever changing rotation of local art. There are no happy hours or quiet times here, so if you're the type of person who likes to drink alone and out of public view, this isn't your spot. Plus, if you're that person, there's a very real chance you're not going to be the type that wants to risk getting got by the rhythm (and make no doubt, it will get you), which generally kicks off right when the bar's doors open at 10pm. Early in the week drinkers will need another spot too, as Medusa is only open Wednesday through Saturday.

Midtown II

122 S. 11th St.
Phone: 215-627-6452

First, a toast to Midtown IV. You were a great little bar in back of a mostly shitty diner on the 2000 block of Chestnut. Before shows at the First Unitarian Church from artists as diverse as Shellac, Raekwon of Wu Tang Clan, elfin yodeler Joanna Newsom or the country leanings of famous offspring Justin Townes Earle, we could rely on you for cold suds and surly service. We'd heard there was toxic mold in the ceiling, but cared not. We'd heard about the rats, too, but it mattered little. We loved you. You were a staple. Now, sadly, you're gone.

The diner was bought by restaurateur Stephen Starr, who changed it into a not bad, somewhat reasonably priced Mexican restaurant called El Rey. The bar is now the very chichi Ranstead Room, which serves some of the most expensive-but-worth-it cocktails in the city. And even though no one in their right, sober mind would argue that this isn't a change for the better, sometimes, in the twilight hours, I shed a single tear for Midtown IV, romanticizing what once was.

Midtown II is still open, and has been since 1974. It too has a bar, and that bar makes losing the dump in the back of IV a tad more palatable. While II is known more for the diner that people from the nearby gayborhood, burnouts, and the all-around blotto hit up after a big night out on the town than for its quaint bar next door (they share a door, actually), the bar is actually a quiet old establishment with boasts some good-natured, ancient barmaids who will actually call you "hon" when they slide your $2 happy hour draft across the bar. There's also a MegaTouch machine at the end of the bar, which a portly, balding waiter from the diner side is very proud to hold a number of records on. Should you pop a few dollars in it, he'll be over in a flash to check up on what you're playing, and will leave his tables in the lurch should it look like you might challenge his immortality on Boxxi Blitz or Word Dojo.

Oscar's Tavern
1524 Sansom St.
Phone: 215-972-9938

Dive Bar Rating

Located between the two major thoroughfares of Chestnut and Walnut, the one-lane downtown section of tiny Sansom was, just a few short years ago, less a street than a back alley for businesses to place their dumpsters in. Save for the occasional jazz great tooting his horn at Chris' Jazz Café and chi-chi Mexican food at restaurateur Stephen Starr's El Vez, there wasn't much going on.

Not so anymore, as Sansom has become kind of a Restaurant Row. Iron chef Jose Garces has two high-end spots on the street, and the posh, newly remodeled Oyster House is the definition of sleek. Zavino serves up gourmet pizza just a few short steps from the overpriced Vietnamese bahn mi sandwiches at ritzy Sampan. A sushi bar, Raw, offers some of the freshest fish in the city and a few doors down from it, Capogiro makes some of the finest gelato you'll ever suck down your gullet.

And then there's Oscars, a nod to the no-frills Sansom of yester-year: dingy, dank, dour, somewhat smelly, and absolutely stripped of any kind of glamour. But don't let that look discourage you—this is one of the friendliest dives in the city, with a festive atmosphere and atypically friendly (for Philly) wait staff. Dance parties often break out in the narrow lane separating red stools and red leather booths at the bar's front, and in back, packed tables placed closely together force you to make new friends with the other jolly drunks. A jukebox which seems to feature either the Isley Brother's album *Eternal* or anything AC/DC on constant repeat says something about how diverse the bar's clientele is. The place also features a healthy (again, for Philly) racial mix, and your barstool neighbor may be a douchebag lawyer type loosening his tie after work, a Phillies die-hard decked out in Chase Utley jersey, Philles cap and Oakley sunglasses, or a withering wino who has bustled enough change on the street to come in for some suds.

The home of the all-the-time 23-ounce, $3.25 beer, the prices at Oscar's are also a nod to the Sansom of yesteryear. They also have an affordable, not-half-bad menu which features Philly staples like the cheesesteak, but also respectable pierogies, mozzarella sticks with marinara, thick, greasy onion rings and huge sausages, all of which engender warm feelings for the place, particularly for the steadfast regulars willing to fight for it. And how. A couple years back, *Philadelphia* magazine's Victor Fiorillo stopped by Oscars and had a glass of Maker's Mark that he thought tasted a little off. He reported this to the State Police's Bureau of Liquor Control Enforcement (which actually exists), and they confiscated six bottles from Oscar's. After testing, they determined the bottles were "contaminated," meaning they were watered down or, worse, Oscar's was serving rotgut out of top shelf bottles. The reaction wasn't the mass exodus you might expect from patrons who felt justifiably jilted. Instead, it imbued tons of support for Oscar's from drinkers who wondered aloud why the hell anyone would order top shelf in a place like this anyway.

After Phillies games, patrons, cooks and bartenders at Oscar's often head out onto narrow, now-posh Sansom to play wiffle ball. They use parked cars as bases, and dodge the ones coming up the street. If Fiorillo ever comes back around, they'll no doubt break out a few real bats.

Paddy's Old City Pub

228 Race St.
Phone: 215-627-3532

Dive Bar Rating

"The first thing you notice upon entering Paddy's Pub is its charm. It has none." So go the first two lines in an *Inquirer* review declaring Paddy's "the worst bar in Philadelphia." And how. Vietnamese immigrants play Russian roulette in the basement, while bums masturbate in the bar's back alley next to gasoline-filled barrels. Paddy's even offers safe haven for underage drinkers. On the bright side, "stabbings are down," though they still happen with alarming frequency, according to the bar's owners.

But wait. The above is about the fictional Paddy's Pub, from the uproariously funny FX hit *It's Always Sunny in Philadelphia*. And though in real life Paddy's isn't near as big a shit hole, the owners don't seem too upset about the association. They sell shirts that read "It's Always Sunny in Paddy's" on the back, and general manager Lauren says they've seen a slight uptick in business since the show began.

The folks spurred to go into the real Paddy's by "the Gang," as the show's trio of Mac, Dennis and Charlie lovingly refer to themselves, will find the only bar in Old City that's been around since the 1914 census. The walls reveal this history, as they are covered in a thick coat of second-hand gunk from decades of smoking, which continues to this day. Paddy's also allows pets, and you're liable to see a dog sitting close to the window or on the barstool next to you on any given night.

The place has its share of salty regulars, and as the name suggests, a fair number of them are Irish. They make for good, drunken conversation. The greatest thing about Paddy's may, in fact, be this drunken old guard, and that they're allowed to smoke inside a place no bigger than a shoe box. Both seem to be why Paddy's isn't overrun by the army of douche that stalks Old City on weekends.

Pen & Pencil

1522 Latimer St.
Phone: 215-731-9909

Depending who you ask, the Pen & Pencil is either the oldest press club in America or "the place I score coke." I don't know about the latter, but the P&P stays open late and is, perhaps unsurprisingly, a hotbed for those employed in the restaurant industry, who come to this speakeasy to imbibe until three in the morning.

Located in a back alley with an easy-to-miss glowing P&P behind a tinted window to mark its entrance, you have to be a member to drink here. Membership costs $40 for the year, and with it you'll have access to the many stellar events the club holds. Well, stellar if you're into long Q&As by grizzled journalists with Philadelphia's mayor, authors like Buzz Bissinger or Pete Dexter stopping by to give a talk about their latest tomes, or food bloggers, chefs, and restaurateurs heading up a panel on the impact of new media on the food industry. It's all heady, interesting stuff. It also happens to be off the record (not unlike most of what goes down at P&P), and chances are you'll never see the featured writers, politicians or whomever in a more candid light.

At the bar's entrance, you'll find old typewriters stacked on shelves. The art on the walls changes regularly and is most often photos by some hotshot newspaper photographer from the days when quality mattered and not any yahoo with a point and click considered himself the next Annie Leibovitz. For the longest time, one of Sarah Solfa's "The Regulars" has been on display. (See: McGlinchey's.) Behind a rectangular bar most nights sits longtime barkeep Danny. Outfitted in tuxedo shirt and vest, Danny is hard of hearing and has two giant hearing aides to prove it. He will more than likely ask you to repeat your order. On a tiny table off to the side of the bar, hotdogs steep in a crock pot; they're referred to affectionately as "crock dogs." (Or is it cautiously?) Whichever, they're not for the faint of heart, and an ever-changing, somewhat-pricey menu is also on hand should you request it. And you should, as some of these authors can talk and talk and talk.

Raven Lounge

1718 Sansom St.
Phone: 215-840-3577

Dive Bar Rating

There are a lot of questions that will forever go unanswered. Where is Jimmy Hoffa? Who shot JFK? What if God was one of us? Now let's add another: *What the hell is going on at Raven Lounge?*

Depending on the night, Raven could be hosting a dance party, karaoke, a hip-hop live show, a goth picnic, a pole dancing competition, a standup comedy night, Jewish Quizzo, sword swallowers, fire-eaters, or arm wrestling championships. You name it, it's goin' down.

Such odd eclecticism would surely make Edgar Allan Poe, the author of the narrative poem the bar is named after, proud. So too would the black walls, black bar and black carpet. The whole place is black, in fact, save for a brick-backed wall behind the booze. As such, Raven is dark. Tiny bursts of neon or the occasional black light are all you'll have to illuminate your copy of "The Raven," should you choose to read it here. No one will stare, or even be able to, if they want to.

Late nights and on weekends, depending on the event, Raven turns from a smelling-of-disinfectant dive into a dance club. Bartenders here consider themselves "soldiers of inebriation" whose solitary mission is to fight off your sobriety one cocktail or beer at a time. Domestics will run you $3 during happy hour, and go up somewhat steeply as the crowd switches over and the vibe changes from quiet dive to loud romper room. Raven doesn't serve food, but conveniently will let you order delivery from the numerous restaurants located within a few short blocks. They even provide the takeout menus.

I suggest you order a chocolate milkshake from venerable diner Little Pete's, then buy a shot of bourbon from one of the soldiers of inebriation and dump it in the shake. Repeat a few times. Later in the night, as you're doubled over the toilet, tickle the back of your throat with a raven's feather, heave violently, and then puke your face off. While doing so, scream "Nevermore!" repeatedly at top volume. What I've just described will, no doubt, soon be on the Raven's calendar of events.

Society Hill Hotel

301 Chestnut St.
Phone: 215-923-3711

Dive Bar Rating

Reading the customer reviews of the Society Hill Hotel on any website—Yelp, Trip Advisor, etc.—is a good way to entertain yourself for a few minutes. You'll get gems like this: "By far the worst hotel in which [sic] I ever slept;" "There was somebody else's PUBIC HAIRS on the bathroom floor;" "The worst living conditions I have ever been in (and I grew up in section 8 housing). The place should be condemned and burned."

A bit harsh, no? Well, who knows? Because like most Philadelphian's, I've never stayed in the hotel, which has been around since 1830. However, the things that make a dive bar great—a bit of curmudgeonly service, a dingy atmosphere, shit talk from a weary regular, even pubic hair on the bathroom floor—are the same things you don't want in the place where you're ultimately going to lay your head, so all the complaints make sense, I suppose.

While weary travelers may have their concerns about staying in the hotel, these concerns do not apply to the bar the hotel sits atop of, a pure, no-frills dive-y gem, stocked with pub favorites Boddingtons, Guinness, Yuengling, and McSorleys on tap. The place is run by Bob Bannon, a fixture in the Philadelphia music—playing drums in Black Landlord, whose singer Maxx also works here—and bar scene, where he's been a fixture at Society Hill for the past six years. (Fun fact: he even played drums for Flock of Seagulls for a short bit.) His attitude is vintage Philly. "Ask me for something foo foo, and I'm going to give you a bottle of Budweiser and a shot of Jack Daniels," he once told a local foodie website.

Bannon probably serves lots of bottles of Bud on the weekend here, when the neighborhood the Hotel is located in, Old City, becomes a playground for popped collars, *Entourage/Sex and the City* types and general douchebaggery. But during the day and most weeknights, there's not a better dive to grab a drink in this part of town. The interior is all dark wooden floors, with about fifteen or so tables to match. The bar is elegant and sturdy at the same time. They just don't make them like this anymore. Or like Bannon.

Tattooed Mom

530 South St.
Phone: 215-546-0316

Dive Bar Rating

There was a time when Philadelphia's South Street was an epically cool place to hang. In the '80s, it was a haven for punk and new wave, and venues like JC Dobb's featured bands like Nirvana, Tool, and Pearl Jam before they broke big. The street was a bastion of artists and the city's freak-set. It was our Beale, our Sixth, our Bourbon, but with fewer tourists.

You'd never know any of this walking down South now, as the street has truly become a living ode to amateur drinkers, late-adopters, and out-of-towners without much of a clue. Gone are record stores like Tower and Spaceboy (Repo, god bless it, still hangs tough). Replacing them are a tacky store called Condom Kingdom (if you're using novelty condoms to spice up your sex life *you're doing it wrong*), a dirty Dairy Queen that seems to always be out of what you want to order, copious bars for assholes and their asshole friends and what can best be described as boutiques that sell clothes to hookers. (Although, that might be an insult to hookers.)

In the middle of it all is Tattooed Mom, an oasis of sanity in a sea of tacky. The bottom floor of the bar is painted lime green from wall to ceiling, and cozy vintage couches are strewn about in a room about half the size of a basketball court. The bartenders, waiters, and waitresses are all much cooler than you, but kind enough to not rub it in your face. Order a PBR pounder and they'll run their heroine-chic, tatted and pierced frames back behind the bar to retrieve it. Depending on the time of day, it may only cost you a dollar. That sounds absurdly low, and it is. But, like house odds at a casino, Tattooed Mom will get you in the end, as they know you'll order three at the special price, all the while cemented to a cozy couch, thumb of God pressed delicately on your forehead. Before you leave, you'll have had plenty more, maybe a shot of Beam thrown in for good, woozy measure.

Happy hour is the draw here, to be sure, and different specials beckon each day. Taco Tuesday features beef or bean tacos for $1.25 a piece, and both versions are damn good. (Especially washed down with dollar Pabst.) For dessert, you'll be happy to suck on one of the dozens of Dum

Dums scattered on each of the tables. Next to them are tiny little party favors—fake tattoos, plastic rings, fortune fish. Upstairs, you'll find two pool tables that never seem to be empty, and the lime green paint used downstairs is replaced by no paint at all. Instead years and years of graffiti cover every inch of wall, floor, and ceiling. Tiny bumper cars to sit in take the place of the cozy couches below, and good news, you're likely to not come back down without hearing a song off the GZA's *Liquid Swords*, which lives in a jukebox that's separate from all the Descendents and Lagwagon-era pop-punk you'll hear downstairs.

Tritone

1508 South St.
Phone: 215-545-0475

Dive Bar Rating

When the Dead Milkmen sang, "I guess I'll just hang out/ On Broad and South/ Livin' on my intuition" in the song "Nutrition" off their 1985 breakthrough album *Big Lizard In My Backyard*, it's fun to imagine they'd just gotten out of a show at the Tritone, even though the place wouldn't open for another decade and a half.

In the summer of 2001, Rick D., a pillar of Philly's punk and music scene, who had booked legendary shows at old haunts like Firenze Tavern, JC Dobbs and Upstairs at Nick's and was responsible for bringing Green Day and Nirvana to town for the first time, bought what would become Tritone from his then bosses at Bob & Barbara's, where he was working as a bartender. B&B had just expanded into a second room, and so its owners no longer felt the need to keep their bar across the street, Bennies, open. So they sold the place to Rick D. and his buying partner Dave Rogers, and the two turned the place into a go-to room for up-and-coming local acts, and, surprisingly, a spot to catch jazz. "I wanted to make something diverse so you'd never know what you were going to get when you walked in. I didn't necessarily intend to get so much into avant jazz, but I'm thrilled we did because the best musicians in the world are coming to my club," Rick told *Philadelphia Weekly* just after the club opened.

Sadly, a heart attack took Rick D.'s life in April of '07, sending shock waves throughout the Philly music scene. Fortunately, Tritone lives on through its ripped chairs, crimson lights, and friendly but surly service from fried-brained burnouts behind the bar who will happily slide a $2.50 citywide special across the bar to you. Speaking of fried: a vast selection of fried foods have always been a staple of Tritone. There are fried catfish nuggets, fried pickles and deep fried candy bars for dessert. If you'd like to go off the well warn fried path, Tritone does an underrated gumbo of the day that's pretty damn good, too.

Best jukeboxes

Oscar's Tavern

Pop Pop's II

Queen of Sheba II

BJ Lounge

Billie's Boomer Lounge

Friendly Lounge

Pen & Pencil

Tattooed Mom

Westbury Bar

261 S. 13th St.
Phone: 215-546-5170

Located smack dab in the middle of Philadelphia's gayborhood, The Westbury is where twinks, bears, bottoms and tops of all races, colors and creeds get together to sip one of the city's most underrated selections of fine beer and do really gay things together like … watch Sportscenter.

There's seriously a lot of beer here, everything Philadelphia foodies have come to expect from high-end gastro pubs like The Standard Tap in trendy Northern Liberties and Kraftwork in Fishtown can be had here, and often for a few dollars less. They also have what seems like every beer Rogue ever bottled and loads of variety from other specialty brewers, with locally brewed Dock Street sitting proudly next to imports like Fuller's of London. Magic Hat, Flying Fish, Dogfish head … you get the picture.

But slamming classy crafts next to positively delightful men hotly debating why, at 50 percent of the city's population, there isn't a homosexual club exclusively marketed to black males in Philadelphia like there is in Atlanta and New York isn't the only draw here. It's also what's above the bar. Westbury is on the ground floor of one of Philly's most notoriously bad-rep hotels, the Parker Spruce, where burnouts, junkies and the just plain snake bitten go when the thought of another night on the streets isn't an option. (No ID required. Cash is fine.) The police have described the place as "a hub of desperation and crime for forever" and civic leaders have demanded that the Fire Department or Philadelphia Licenses and Inspections look into the living conditions of those who take up temporary residence in the place, labeling it "a derelict building."

The bad PR the hotel has garnered over the last forty years comes courtesy of what spills out it's front door, clearly inebriated and sometimes-high individuals who ask passersby for "bus fare" or "something to eat." Tenants at the hotel sometimes work their way down to The Westbury, which can get interesting, but which sadly has become more of a rarity these days, as the bar got a spit shine and a fresh coat of paint in late '09 when it was bought by new owners, who work a bit harder than the old owners at keeping out the riff raff. The new owners have been good for something else too: I'm told by a friend who delivers beer to the bar that the storage room in the basement used to be the scariest place in the city, filled with giant rats, dirty mattresses and old furniture from the Parker Spruce. Now, after the clean-up, you can drink your Rogue Dead Guy Ale down there without worrying that it might actually kill you.

Live Music

El Bar

Fiume

Bob & Barbara's

Medusa Lounge

Friendly Lounge

SOUTH PHILLY

1201 Bar

1201 S. 28th St.
Phone: 215-339-9282

Dive Bar Rating

I'd probably gone past the 1201 Bar a few thousand times before I actually knew it was there. You see, while I have a friend who lives in the area, the road the bar is located on, Grays Ferry, a large thoroughfare that connects commuters from West Philly into Center City via the Grays Ferry Bridge, is one of the few streets in Philly that's not pedestrian friendly. Or friendly, period. Legendary hardscrabble *Daily News* columnist Pete Dexter was nearly beaten to death by men wielding baseball bats in a Grays Ferry bar not too far from 1201. They broke his pelvis, and it took sixty stitches to close his wounds. In addition, the sign-free outside of the 1201 looks abandoned, and to the south and east is Point Breeze, a lower class African American neighborhood that's plagued by crime and drug trafficking, and to the north and west is a Pathmark grocery store, and a McDonald's with a drive-thru (a rare thing in Philly, actually). So, you can understand out why I wouldn't think there was anything here, let alone a pretty cool dive.

In fact, the 1201 Bar has been on this corner of 28th and Grays Ferry since 1984. Its patrons, like the neighborhood around it, are mostly black, and Michael Jackson and old soul hits pour loudly and generously out of the Touch Tunes digital jukebox. There are tightly ridged grooves cut into its balsa wood walls, which are the color of football leather. Mondays are free pretzel night, and everything on the bottom shelf is always $2. There's also a giant bottle of Jacquin's rum behind the bar. Jacquin's is a local distiller of rum, vodka and assorted other spirits, and nearly everything they make is cloyingly sweet, but people seem to really dig their rum here, as it, along with a big jug of E&J brandy, gets tipped quite a bit. There's also a pool table in the back room, surrounded by a few pool trophies. The bar does robust business selling beer to go to folks on foot from Point Breeze. At $2.50 for a forty of Hurricane, it's worth the trek.

12 Steps Down

831 Christian St.
Phone: 215-238-0379

Dive Bar Rating

My bartender friend Pete is always going on about how bars just don't have cool names anymore. A quick scan of new Philly spots bears this out: Time, Tria, Noche, Noble. And don't you dare get him started on the recently opened "Bar." "It's like naming your dog 'Dog!' C'mon!"

However, Pete has no problem with South Philly's 12 Steps Down. And clever though its name may be, this basement dive (it is literally 12 steps down into the place) off of Philly's legendary Italian market certainly has something to teach the newbies. Like how to make a whipass, spicy and vodka-packed Bloody Mary for $2. And stiff mimosas for the same price. If cheap brunch-time drinks aren't your thing, 12 Step has you covered too, with an incredibly ambitious selection of suds for such a dark little hole in the ground: Young's Double Chocolate Stout, Ommegang Three Philosophers, Flying Fish Exit 1, and Dogfish Head Aprihop, just to name a few.

The food at 12 Steps is similarly impressive, including hand cut fries served with a smoked ketchup (perfectly complimenting the smoking going on all around you) or aioli. Their PBR battered chicken fingers are the perfect drunk food, but if you're looking for something a little more sophisticated to accompany your high-brow brew, they've also got a crispy calamari salad that ain't half bad and a stellar chicken cobb sandwich.

A couple of pool tables and a big screen TV fill out the green-walled basement, which feels like your buddy's below ground apartment, albeit with a fully-stocked bar. Friendly bartenders add to the cozy feeling, and, though underground, the bar's ample space and room for plenty make tolerating the smoke easier. And if it doesn't, you can take those 12 steps back up.

Big Charlie's Saloon

11th and McKean Sts.
No Phone

Dive Bar Rating

Can a bar be a dive if it's won an Emmy? Because when you dial up @ bigcharlies on twitter, you'll see a picture of that coveted television prize, standing proudly on the bar at Big Charlie's Saloon.

In 2004, the NFL Network brought then Kansas City Chiefs (and onetime Eagles) coach Dick Vermeil and a group of his players to Big Charlie's to film a segment, which wound up winning an Emmy. In addition to the award, what makes Big Charlie's unique is that, in the middle of Eagles' country, where our citizens bleed green and routinely curb stomp fans of other teams brazen enough to wear non-Eagles gear, the place is a shrine to all things Kansas City Chiefs (it's referred to as Arrowhead East by its regulars). On the bar's walls and shelves, you'll find old Chiefs' jerseys, posters, helmets, footballs signed by Chiefs' players, newspaper clippings, helmets, bobble head dolls, a three-foot cigar store KC Indian, press photos and basically anything else emblazoned with a giant red KC or an arrowhead. On Sundays, the bar televises Kansas City Chiefs' games.

Behind the bar, next to that Emmy, you'll find old black and white photos of boxers punching it out, a Captain Air smoke purification system (smoking's still allowed here) and Kansas City Chiefs' beer steins hanging perilously from the ceiling. There are a couple fridges and a microwave in plain sight in the tiny open-air kitchen caddy-corner from the bar, which serves up hot dogs on game day, though is closed most nights. Past it is a back room, which is a virtual Kansas City Chiefs museum, reflecting what Big Charlie Staico, who opened the place in the mid-'70s, dreamt for this bar to be; namely, a safe haven where fans of the Chiefs could let their freak flags fly in peace. In the bar's front room, just off the entrance on the right hand side, hangs a painting in memoriam to Big Charlie, who died in 1983. Charlie's son Paul runs the business now, and despite being a Philly native, is a die-hard Chiefs fan just like his pop. Hail to the Chief(s).

Bonnie's Capistrano

1503 S. 13th St.
Phone: 215-462-7282

Dive Bar Rating

The blizzard-like snow was bringing in people searching for a place to plop down for a drink and seek shelter. Some had grocery bags. Some just wanted to get out of the house to be around company for a cheap beer and a smoke. All wanted to complain about the lousy weather. A young, cute schoolteacher was worried about who might mosey in and catch her smoking. Whole weeks of school had been canceled already, and she'd spent most of that time at Bonnie's waiting for it all to end. The snow, I mean. Not the world. Though it sure did feel like that, as the winter of '09-'10 was already officially Philly's worst ever, with the largest snowfall the city had ever seen in one season, and it kept ... coming ... down. What at one point seemed quaint—the streets romantically covered in puffy white snow—was now a major league pain in the balls. People were turning bitter. They were beating one another in the streets over the few parking spaces that had been dug out. Things were getting ugly. Fortunately, there were places like Bonnie's, which literally kept the city going during the winter that wouldn't end.

The inside of the place looks like the set of a restaurant from an '80s sitcom. Fake green plants are strewn about, and glasses hang above the bar. The dark walls remain unadorned for the most part, and there's a dining room in back that goes largely unused. In other words, nuttin' too fancy. The bartender is quiet but efficient, lighting his pipe and taking a puff here and there between pours. Bonnie herself is here most nights, a talkative Italian who doesn't suffer fools gladly, but is kind as they come to those who check their pretense at the door.

This is an old school South Philly hangout, and on a night without a blizzard, lots of Italians from the neighborhood come in to sip $2 lagers and $3 whiskeys. One or two of the regulars might shoot you a dirty look, but that's part of the place's appeal. And don't worry—if they get too salty, Bonnie will straighten them out.

Brothers Two

1428 W. Ritner St.
Phone: 215-468-9869

"There are no strangers here. Just friends that have not met." So it is written on a sign on the wall at Brothers Two. And you get the distinct feeling they mean it. (And not just because the sign is painstakingly written in calligraphy.) All around the rectangle shaped bar, old acquaintances and new friends alike are sharing laughs, drinks, and pizza. The owner has ordered several large pies from the pizza shop up the street, and anyone who buys a drink is welcome to a slice or two.

The close-knit guy friends here all mercilessly break one another's balls about anything under the sun. "No more pizza for you. You're getting a gut." "He can't be on my [dart] team. He couldn't hit the broad side of a barn." "We're closed, go away!" to a friend who's just walked in. This is immediately followed by fist bumps and bear hugs. The large Touch Tunes jukebox affixed to the back wall is getting an AC/DC workout. "Shoot To Thrill," "For Those About To Rock," "Thunderstruck." The guys break one another's balls about this too, as anyone who steps up to feed dollars to the machine is warned not to play any "dumb shit."

There are a couple Dodge City digital poker games around the place, but folks are too busy with darts to pay them much mind. The back wall of the bar is a tight squeeze, and there's not a lot of wiggle room to adjust your barstool. Customers sitting in the middle back need to have a gargantuan bladder or not break the seal too soon into a night of hammering back Buds, or there's going to be an accident. A couple of the bigger bodies in the room are told to "think thin" when squeezing between the bar and wall.

Burg's Lounge

1200 S. 21st St.
Phone: 215-271-6627

Dive Bar Rating

The Point Breeze neighborhood of South Philly isn't exactly where you'd want to find yourself late at night. Boarded up buildings abound, and open air drug dealing and street crime is common. For decades, this lower-to-middle-class black neighborhood has withered on the vine, and the decades of neglect and decay are on display everywhere.

Still, over the last few years, the neighborhood—like many in Philly, such as Northern Liberties, Fishtown, and pockets of the West—has been dusted off, and a fresh coat of paint plastered on it. The Sidecar Bar and Grille opened up, and fought hard to get something previously unheard of in Point Breeze: sidewalk dining. With Sidecar came other bars and restaurants. As a result, PB is looking up, attracting young white couples to buy its dirt-cheap properties and fix them up. Now, talk of gentrification and the higher property taxes that come with it are a hot topic in the area, with the Point Breeze lifers expressing real worry about whether or not they are going to be displaced.

This might very well be the topic of conversation if you stumble into Burg's Lounge, a black-owned Point Breeze watering hole that's been open since 1977 and, it seems, hasn't been renovated since. Attached to the non-descript, somewhat decrepit exterior, are large posters advertising $2 40-ounce Hurricane malt liquor. Inside, the place is much nicer than you'd expect, with clean blue and white tiled floors casting a bit of light alongside a dark shotgun bar, Christmas lights hanging above a long mirror behind it. There's Strike Master shuffleboard bowling in back, and a Mega Touch machine up front next to a Touch Tunes jukebox that proudly boasts that T.I. is its most played artist.

The bartender talks inconspicuously into the Blue Tooth in her ear, and isn't interested in conversation with customers, the only breaks in her phone chat being to take your order and tell you the total. Occasionally she'll tell a regular she's just become a grandmother. Behind the bar is enough Bacardi to kill a horse—Gold, Silver, 151, regular, coconut, raspberry, limon, orange—and several other brands of rum. An elderly woman walks in, sits down. The bartender, still blabbing into her Blue Tooth, pours her a plastic cup of port wine over ice without asking. Despite several signs around the bar announcing "No Smoking," the old lady lights up, taking puffs between sips of her wine. Maybe Burg's should also think about applying to the city for outdoor seating?

Cookie's Tavern

2654 Alder St.
Phone: 215-271-9487

Dive Bar Rating

Like the Tailhook Tavern in the Great Northeast, Cookie's Tavern in deep South Philly is a military bar. Specifically, it's a Marine bar, as longtime owner James "Daddy Wags" Wagner joined the Corp in '64, where he spent four years, serving two tours in Vietnam and being awarded a Purple Heart. His service and the Corp meant a lot to him, and since the mid-70s, Cookie's Tavern has played host to a gigantic bash commemorating the birth of the Marines, which was started in a Philadelphia bar called Tun Tavern on November 10, 1775. Every year on November 10, the streets around Cookie's are blocked off, and thousands of current and former Marines gather with their families to celebrate by tossing a few back. It remains one of the biggest Marine bashes in the country. While Daddy Wags died of a brain tumor in 2002, the birthday celebration continues on today, with his spirit as guide.

Daddy Wags's daughter Marion now owns Cookie's, and she runs a tight ship, if she'll please excuse the Navy pun. Inside the smoke choked bar, grizzled Marine Corp youngins cozy up next to old heads from the neighborhood and veterans of foreign wars. There's a sign behind the bar that reads "We don't call 911," and you get the feeling it's no joke, and not just because one of the main bartenders at Cookie's, Big Mike, is deaf and therefore couldn't call even if he wanted to.

Dotted around the bar are is some Semper Fi memorabilia as well as homage's to Philly sports teams. They keep it bright in here, which can be distracting if it's late and you've had more than your share—it *constantly* looks like last call. Some say it's so Big Mike can show off his always freshly manicured nails. (He's even talked about getting diamonds pressed into them.) If that sounds a bit strange for a bar as macho as this one, it is. But Mike is a hulk of a man, and no one is going to fuck with him. Not even a Marine. And if someone does, remember, they don't call 911.

DiNic's Tavern

1528 Snyder Ave.
Phone: 215-336-2333

Dive Bar Rating

There are two things you should commit to memory before heading to DiNic's:

One, it's not *that* DiNic's. This should be easy, as DiNic's in the Reading Terminal Market is famous for its gourmet pulled pork sandwiches. With too-tall stacks of succulent pig topped high with broccoli rabe and sharp provolone, *that* DiNic's has been featured on the Food Network and in countless magazine features on the glories of Philly food culture. So though the sign at *this* DiNic's reads DiNic's Beef Pork Tavern, it's not *that* DiNic's.

Two, now that you know what DiNic's you're actually in, don't sit by the door, as every ten minutes or so, a junkie, grifter, or someone looking to borrow from, lie to or cheat you will be walking through it. As the person sitting closest to the entrance, you will be their mark. The first half dozen scammers will more than likely be taken care of by the bartender as a courtesy, her screams of "GET THE FUCK OUTTA HERE, YA BUM!" a gentle hand to help you, the guy who sat by the door like a woefully obvious noob.

And a thing about that bartender: even had you not sat by the door, she'd still know that you're not a regular because DiNic's is mainly populated by a handful of hardcore drinkers who spend morning, noon and night here, thus you're stopping by will not go unnoticed. People will stare. Some might even ask what you're doing here. You will be scoped out, studied. Some might even presume you're an officer of the law. If all that makes you feel uneasy, I suggest you drink more.

Luckily, DiNic's makes that easy, with cheap cans of not-fancy swill stocked cold, and a decent selection of cheap hard stuff that'll make you feel a little less self-conscious. Both the bar's interior and its prices haven't changed since the Nixon administration. Smoking is allowed, and everyone here does, and years of secondhand smoke have tarred the faux-wood paneled walls and ceiling. While the place is primarily old school, there are a few modern flourishes, such as an Internet jukebox and a pair of Touchscreen video game consoles.

Once they've warmed to you, the regulars will drunkenly talk baseball with the seriousness of religion. The men's bathroom in back may or may not have a door, but no one seems to mind. The bartender will graciously announce when someone's heading back to drop a deuce, and will warn the other regulars not to head back there lest they catch a peep of something unsightly. On second thought, maybe you should sit next to the front door.

SOUTH PHILLY

PHILADELPHIA'S BEST DIVE BARS

The Dive

947 E. Passyunk Ave.
Phone: 215-465-5505

Dive Bar Rating

Chances are you'll never meet a more excitable person than John Klein, owner of the Bella Vista dive called The Dive. And that's a good thing, because that guy would be exhausting. Klein himself is a fast talker, with tons of ideas, many of them pretty damn stellar. Like opening a bar that lives up to its name.

The Dive is unkempt and smoke choked, and you're welcome to bring your dog if you don't mind risking giving the old pooch lung cancer. On the other hand, you can feed him free pizza during happy hour, and that's always a plus. Upstairs there's pool and darts, DJs and live music. All of this attracts a pretty regular crowd, who cram into one of The Dive's three floors to drink cheap beer, smoke the night away, play Xbox or watch Adult Swim or *The Simpsons*, both of which seem to be on the TV downstairs on an unending loop. Free form open mike nights draw big crowds too. Pounders of PBR and Schlitz will cost you eight quarters.

A couple years back, Klein had trouble with Philly's Licenses and Inspections, generally known as the humorless mafia-like arm of city government. Bella Vista, as you can possibly surmise by the name, is a quaint, sexy nook of the otherwise not quaint or sexy South Philly. The Dive is right next door to a wildly acclaimed gastro-pub, Royal Tavern, and so the theory goes that some neighbor, unhappy with a place called The Dive moving in, pulled some strings with his boys working for the city to harass ole Good Idea Klein. They did this by ticketing him every which way but loose for things as arcane as not having three emergency lights in his bottom floor (which is a whopping 600 square feet). It got to a point where he couldn't even go out anymore, lest he be reminded of his troubles—search, he would, for proper emergency lighting in new multi-million dollar restaurants, and justifiably freak when he found they weren't up to "code" either. Fortunately, he weathered the city government shit storm and now, several thousands of dollars and lost hours of sleep later, The Dive has been left alone to do what it does best: be uncompromisingly and gloriously dive-y.

Dolphin Tavern

1539 S. Broad St.
Phone: 215-467-1752

Dive Bar Rating

A few years back, the Boston Red Sox were in town to play an interleague series with the Phillies. This, of course, meant that swarms of Boston fans descended upon our fair city, as Red Sawx Nation is a notoriously travel-happy bunch. After game one of the series, a dozen or so Sawx fans were lured into the Dolphin Tavern by both its close proximity to Citizen's Bank Park and by what it says next to the front door: "Dancers Revue." If they were on the hunt for a real skin bar—which they said they were—then they had definitely come to the wrong place, as the Dolphin Tavern is where punk rock comes to take off its clothes. (And punk rock keeps its nipples hidden under electric tape.) These Boston fans were decidedly *not punk rock*.

Behind a long black, rectangle bar that runs the length of half the room are three, equally spaced, stand alone black platform stages. Intermittently, starting at nine, only on Friday and Saturday nights, the dancers make their way out slowly and shake what their mama gave them to music dictated by the patrons dropping coin in the jukebox. This could be anything from country to Def Leppard, rap to Slayer. No matter what's spinnin', the dancers abide. Tattooed, pierced, maybe a tad past their prime or with something extra around the middle, these ladies likely wouldn't make the cut at other, more hoity digs, mainly because shaved heads don't fly at those kinds of joints.

Still, you won't experience any of the typical strip club traps of, say, Delilah's—the lap dance hard sell, the fake wanting to know about you, the rock-hard, veiny basketball-sized cans and spray tans—at Dolphin's. And that's part of what makes the place so unique (well, that and the fetish porn DVDs up for grabs in the claw machine.) This isn't the spot for the suburban husband looking to escape his wife and kids for a night of release. This is where that guy gets cut. Or, at the very least, mocked mercilessly. The dancers here won't be sticking a vacuum hose into your back pocket. Most of the regulars ignore them, in fact, flicking a crinkled one-dollar bill here and there when the mood hits them.

The dancers aren't the only attraction, of course, as there are drinks to be had. The beer selection at Dolphin is scant (Bud and Miller, that's about it), so go with something hard. Back past the bar is a dance floor that, in its heyday, used to light up "Billy Jean" style, but now has been reduced to a few flickering burps. There are pool tables too, and a tiny raised stage that used to feature live music. Back by the bar's entrance, if you're lucky, you'll see Mama. White hair, chain-smoking, sipping on something mixed with punch, she owns the joint, and ask anyone who's been to the Dolphin and they'll tell a different story about her—she's in her 90s, she used to dance, she's the last surviving member of her family and abysmally sad. That's why she drinks. Truth is, you don't want to know her truth. It would ruin it.

Speaking of ruining it. It's nine o'clock and the dancers have made it to the starting blocks. The Bostonians, squares that they are, are none too pleased. "Oh. Moi. Gawd," One of them says. "That one looks like Tony Soprano's sistah!" People all around the bar turn and shoot him nasty looks. Not to worry, though, Janice can handle these chumps herself. "Why don't you get the fuck outta here, ya New Kids on the Block listenin' motherfuckers!" she screams. Phillies: 1. Bo Sox: 0. Don't recall how the actual game went.

Fireside Tavern

2701 S. Marshall St.
Phone: 215-271-7650

Dive Bar Rating

A marquee in the bed of a broken-down truck out front of Fireside Tavern advertises $2 pints of Bud Light. However, this enticement doesn't seem to be luring customers into the place with any consistency, as, the night I was here, there were exactly two people at the bar: a rather large black man and a medium-sized white woman. She was missing one of her front teeth and was wearing what seemed to be a turquoise sports bra. Sitting on the guy's lap, she arched her back, then gave him a deep, open mouth kiss. On the jukebox, Gavin Rosdale, lead singer of Bush, was doing an acoustic solo set to a room full of zombies who clapped politely after he'd puked out his soul singing "Glycerin."

The good news is there's plenty at Fireside to distract you. A 16-ounce PBR will only run you 25 cents more than the $2 Bud Light advertised outside. Along the back exposed brick wall, a shuffleboard bowling game is only 25 cents, too. Next to it is the crème de la crème of all target/hunting games, Big Buck Hunter. It costs more, but also lasts longer. Considering that the couple at the bar is in now full-on PDA mode and the bartender seems to be more amused than disgusted, it's worth the extra scrilla.

There's not much aesthetically striking about Fireside. It wears its Irish pride proudly in this Italian neighborhood, with green everywhere and an Irish flag hanging from the ceiling. Green Tiffany lamps—all without light bulbs—that look like they were purchased at a Bennigan's rummage sale hang above lonely, unused tables. Fireside sells six packs of Twisted Iced Tea for $7, and a cooler by the bathroom is stocked full of the stuff. Should a natural disaster ever strike Philly causing a shortage of Twisted Iced Tea, Fireside would have your back. A 1970s-era Phillies guide printed by the *Inquirer* hangs framed by the doorway. As Gavin Rosdale begins to howl "There's no sex in violence!!!" loudly from the speakers, I walk through it. He's obviously never met the couple at the bar.

Friendly Lounge

1039 S. Eighth St.
Phone: 215-627-9798

Dive Bar Rating

Even on weekends, when the world famous Italian Market is teeming with foodies in search of something exotic to gnash, Friendly Lounge, a mere block away, is quiet. As a matter of fact, the place is seldom crowded, and for some that's the draw. Even when the jukebox is playing, it's at a reasonable volume, and most times the only noise emanating comes from the TV on the back wall between the men's and women's restrooms and the regular's talking to it between drags on their cigarettes.

The owner, Dominick, doesn't mind the low key vibe. He'll tell you that he's burnt out, and even though there's a kitchen in back, it hasn't served food in years, as he is too tired to get the pilots on the stoves and oven lit again. This, it turns out, works in your favor, as Dominick doesn't care one wit whether or not you bring in food from the 9th Street Italian Market. (Tip: Go get a sandwich from Paesano's. You're welcome.)

Dom and his brother Marco took over Friendly in 1971 when their mother died. They brought in go-go dancers back then, and saw an uptick in business because of it for a few years, but ultimately decided to do without them. A photo of a naked pinup sits next to a vintage cash register in homage to those days gone by, and a few other pictures of scantily clad girls doing rope tricks are taped to a mirror behind the bar. And what a gorgeous bar it is, rounded at the edge with a plump leather cushion, perfect for long shifts sitting and sipping in peace.

The dancers may be gone, but that's about the only thing in Friendly that has changed over the years. The signs above each of the bathrooms look straight out of the *Mad Men* prop room, and the brown ceiling and dark wood walls are caked with the tar of decades' worth of secondhand smoke. There's also still a real jukebox here, and in it you'll find greatest hits by the likes of Janis Joplin and Van Morrison. There are even two Billy Joel Greatest Hits collections which, I say without hint of irony, is a beautiful thing.

SOUTH PHILLY

PHILADELPHIA'S BEST DIVE BARS

Grumpy's Tavern

Dive Bar Rating

While Tony, the owner of Grumpy's, only bought the place six years ago, the bar actually has a long and storied history. Before it was called Grumpy's, it was Pinto's, one of the oldest bars in Philadelphia, having been issued one of the first thousand liquor licenses ever in the city. The bar moved to its current location in 1959, and though the place has some modern tweaks, the long shotgun bar and wooden walls are all quite familiar to the old heads in the neighborhood who went to Pinto's back in the day, and continue to come to Grumpy's today.

Though the name may have changed, the prices haven't, as a can of PBR will only set you back $2 all day every day, and a ten ounce can of Bud goes for a mere dollar during Phillies games. Speaking of the Phillies, every year, the regulars here—a mix of young and old Italians from the neighborhood—take in a game at Citizen's Bank Park. It's called Grumpy's Night at the Park.

There's a pool table in the back room, and an upstairs area with extra seating when things begin to get a bit packed, which they do sometimes. Most of the patrons at Grumpy's—whether stopping in all night or grabbing a quick six to go—know one another, and conversations about the merits of everything from Lady Gaga to newly proposed city taxes can and will be debated loudly, especially after a few of whatever special the bar is offering on that particular night (on Mondays it's a can of Bud and a shot of Jameson for $3). You get the feeling the words "I love you, man" get a pretty hefty workout here, an odd thing considering the bar's name.

Nickel's Tavern

2655 S. Second St.
Phone: 215-468-9581

Dive Bar Rating

A quick word to those bars still using those old-timey cloth towel dispensers in their bathrooms: Really? I mean, I know you're all for doing your part for the environment, but the cloth dispenser—with its long, always-damp attached towel hanging low—isn't the way for your bar to go green. In fact, I'd argue it encourages people to not wash their hands.

Nickel's Tavern has a cloth towel dispenser. And like those dispensers, Nickel's is a nasty, nasty joint. There seems to be a wild aggression in the air, with smoke filling the room and an inescapable feeling that everyone in the place won't be happy until they've either fought or fucked with whoever is sitting or standing next to them. Around the rectangular bar, a mostly white, working class crowd dressed almost exclusively in Flyers gear huddle and talk loudly. Red Bull mixed with anything seems to be their drink of choice, and the poor, lone bartender can't keep up with the demand of a fully-packed Saturday night, making her way around, taking one Red Bull and something order at a time, shooting you nasty looks if you try to order out of town. Behind the bar, there is a heating table that is supposed to keep food hot throughout the day. Under metal lids, dirty hot dogs sit for hours, steeping in their own tepid juices. It's irritable bowel syndrome just waiting to happen. Perhaps the Taurine in Red Bull helps kill those nasty parasites?

On the wall, by the food service area is a framed picture of Babe Ruth, which seems odd in a South Philly bar just a stiff walk from where the Phillies play. Next to it hangs a picture of Jim Bunning, former Phillies pitcher, now Republican Senator from Kentucky. At a bar like this, and next to the Bambino, it's hard to tell if the picture of Bunning is meant to memorialize his graceful curveball and perfect game against the hated rival Mets or his attempt as a Senator to cut off unemployment benefits, kick the unemployed off healthcare and deny satellite TV to rural America (an actual proposed bill of his). Either way, it sounds like the actions of a guy who's dried his hands on a few too many disease infested cloth towels, and it's started to infect his brain.

Penns Port Pub

1920 Delaware Ave.
Phone: 215-336-7033

Penns Port Pub is not a pub, but a strip club way the hell out (for Philly) on Delaware Ave, just a hop, skip and jump away from a Target and a Wal-Mart. Most of its business comes from local stevedores who work on the docks, and the bar's hours of operation reflect its blue-collar clientele. They open at 11am for lunch for modest roast beef sandwiches and other fare, and generally close at 7pm during the week, giving the dock workers an hour or two of titty ogling time after they've called it quits for the day. On Saturday, the place is open from 11am to midnight, while it is closed on Sunday, naturally, on account of the Lord.

Where most strip clubs come with that pre-packaged atmosphere featuring the inevitable and awkward sit down with the stripper hoping to hard sell you on a lap dance you can't afford, only to make you feel the fool for declining, the set up at Penns Port is different. The girls here walk out on the square bar that you're sitting at one by one in shifts of three, making their way around while Journey, Loverboy or some other band from the '80s blares loudly from overhead speakers. Dancers with names like Melody, Starr and Horizon will park themselves in front of your beer (insanely cheap for a strip joint), and ask how you're doing. Then they'll thrust their breasts into your face. You give them a dollar. They bend over, and show you the back door. You give them another dollar. Finally, they squat in front of you, pull their underwear aside, and give you a glimpse of roast beef of a different kind. You pay them a third dollar. It might not be illegal, but it certainly is unsanitary. (On second thought, it might be illegal.)

All told, you're basically renting your barstool for $9 an hour as the three women on shift make their rounds to you. Of course, if the prospect of eating your lunch with women's privates inches from your face doesn't interest you, you're more than welcome to sit at one of the booths up front away from the bar, or to play pool in the tacked on backroom. Melody, Starr and Horizon sure are going to miss you terribly, though.

Ray's Happy Birthday Bar

1200 E. Passyunk Ave.
Phone: 215-365-1169

Dive Bar Rating

Have you heard about the renaissance going down on East Passyunk in South Philly? You haven't? Well then, you haven't been reading your *New York Times*, or *Philadelphia Inquirer*. Because if you had, you'd know that East Passyunk is where it's at, with young, small business entrepreneurs opening up vital new shops at an impressive clip alongside the oldsters that have been here for years. An offshoot of this growth are hot bars like the Pub on Passyunk East (POPE), which is packed night in, night out with musicians, artists and the generally hip. Then, down the Avenue a ways, you've got Ray's Happy Birthday Bar, a block north of the Geno's and Pat's Steaks nexus.

It's truly a brilliant idea, putting "Happy Birthday" in the name of your establishment. Because, inevitably, it is someone's birthday, and that someone undoubtedly has friends. Ray's is where they gather. The place opens at seven in the morning, and what's more impressive than that is that there are actually people here when it opens—a popular saying around Ray's is "You can't drink all day if you don't start in the morning." And it's a healthy mix—restaurant industry workers at the tail end of wicked all-night benders, crud-covered sanitation and sewer crews just off the graveyard shift, and old folks hoping that the next shot of Beam will be their last.

Before he took over the bar his father opened in 1938, owner Lou Cappazolli moonlighted in Vegas during the time that the mob and Rat Pack ran it. You get a sense of that in the tone he's set for his place. Smoking is permitted, and boy, do people love to light up here. They love to drink too, and pounders of High Life and PBR are dirt-cheap. So too are mixed drinks, which generally run $5 so long as you're not eyeing the top shelf. What, $5 doesn't seem that inexpensive? Oh, yes, forgot to mention that they serve them in a pint glass.

Those pint glasses can also serve up some pretty tasty craft brews. Ray's consistently has Victory's Hop Devil on tap, and a rotating cast of other nice surprises on draft. Karaoke on Friday nights is a huge draw, and even though most of the drunken masses participating can't carry a tune, it's easy to see why they're here, as it's pretty hard to have a bad time at Ray's (unless you're allergic to smoke). They also sell six packs to go. So sing the old Hank Thompson song with me: "Hey, Mr. Bartender/ Don't you be so slow/ I got time for one more round, and a six pack to go/ Tomorrow mornin's Sunday/ I'm gonna be feelin' low/ So please, please bartender/ I wanna six pack to go."

Rosewood Bar

1417 W. Shunk St.
Phone: 215-336-1335

Dive Bar Rating

The interior of the Rosewood Bar was used as the model for the Mark Wahlberg movie *Invincible*, a modest-sized picture that cast Wahlberg as an everyman who becomes a walk-on player for the Eagles. The movie is actually the true-life story of Vince Papale, a down-and-out guy who'd lost his job as a teacher and had turned to bartending to make ends meet. During the 1976 season, a year that the team was terrible, then-coach Dick Vermeil (played by in the movie by Greg Kinnear) tried to spice things by holding open tryouts for the team. Papale made the cut.

While the interiors for *Invincible* were reconstructed note for note, barstool for barstool, down at the Navy Yard (the exteriors used in the film were of the real Rosewood location, which is located on tiny Shunk Street, next to Oregon and Broad), inside the actual Rosewood, it still looks like they never got past the bicentennial. Around a giant oblong bar, you'll find an older crowd of regulars smoking butts and drinking Buds. Sinatra is the music of choice playing on the honest-to-goodness real jukebox that's also stocked with Tony Bennett, Neil Diamond, Billy Joel, George Strait and Elton John. There are three Celine Dion albums in there too, but the less said about them the better.

The walls of Rosewood are painted bright Phillies' red, and tiny two- and four-top tables cozy up to red leather banquettes on both walls after the bar ends. There's a pool table in back, and a kitchen that I'm told puts out decent slop. (Seafood Sundays are popular.) Don't eat too much, though, or you'll never fit in the restrooms, which are tinier (and wetter) than any you've likely ever been in before.

Triangle Tavern

1338 S. 10th St.
Phone: 215-467-8683

Dive Bar Rating

Melanie Chongolola and her boyfriend David Nestor were out on a date. They'd just finished up a nice meal and wanted to get a quick drink before heading home. Unfortunately, they got a lot more than that. You see, Chongolola and Nestor are an interracial couple; she's black, he's white. They went to the Triangle Tavern, ordered drinks, and paid for their round. While they were enjoying their cocktails, an older man in the corner started mumbling loudly and angrily. Then he started in with the racial slurs. Soon, a fight ensued, barstools were toppled, and Nestor was choked. The cops were called, and they arrived just after the angry man had gotten in a white Cadillac and pulled off. Luckily, Chongolola and Nestor had gotten his license plate number. Turns out the car was registered to James Dachino, the owner of the Triangle Tavern.

Dachino and the regulars at the Triangle Tavern dispute this story, of course. They say Chongolola was rude and already a bit tipsy when she walked into the bar, and that she started the fight and made up the racially charged name-calling. Who to believe in all this is unclear, though what isn't unclear is that the Triangle has been on this particular corner in South Philly since 1933, and wears every bit of its age. Its faux wood walls are dull from cigarette smoke (which is still allowed today), and the prices are pretty reasonable—$3 for a can of Pabst.

The bar gets its name from its odd, triangle shaped bar, on top of which are baskets of still-in-the-shell peanuts available to customers who don't feel like splurging on the Funyuns, Doritos, or Cheez Its for sale in the vending machine next to the front entrance. While there's an old sign advertising roast beef sandwiches, bartender Franny from New Jersey says that the kitchen hasn't been open in a long time. That changes in January, when, she says, they'll use a tiny space in the basement to put out free sausages on Sundays and Monday nights, during football games. Plans for a full menu including mussels and "bar foods" are also coming down the pike, but Franny can't say exactly when.

Franny also can't say exactly where they got the gorgeous mirrored painting of a woman that hangs in the back room behind the bar. It's quintessential '80s, and looks like it was ripped from a Jordache ad. Next to it hangs a painting of the Italian market, which is a stones' throw away from Triangle. Only it's not very Italian anymore, as it's seen an influx of Mexican immigrants over the last few years, many of whom head to the Triangle for after work imbibing. If there are racist shenanigans going down here, they sure don't seem aware of it.

Fishtown Tavern

NORTH PHILLY

FISHTOWN/ NORTHERN LIBERTIES/ PORT RICHMOND/ KENSINGTON/ FAIRMOUNT

Atlantis (The Lost Bar)

2442 Frankford Ave.
Phone: 215-739-4929

A few years back, trouble was brewing (pun intended!) at the venerable Philly brewery Yards. Unhappy with one another, the principle owners decided to split. Tom Kehoe would take the Yards brand name and recipes, while Nancy Barton and her husband Bill would keep the physical building in Kensington so that they could start their own brand, which turned out to be Philadelphia Brewing Company, otherwise known as PBC on bar chalkboards across the city.

PBC has had a bit of cool cache stored up over the last few years, helped all the more by the fact that it employs many a Philly musician. For example, Matador records wunderkind Kurt Vile used to drive a forklift here, and Richie Charles of Clockcleaner, formerly on sweet-ass label Load Records, drives the delivery truck.

Atlantis (The Lost Bar) sits across the street from the PBC brewery, and owners Nancy and Bill can often be found here, usually sipping one of their own stellar beer varieties, whether it be Walt Wit, Newbold IPA, Rowhouse Red or, their most popular, Kenzinger, so named after the neighborhood in which it's brewed. Other special seasonal beers like Fleur De Lehigh and Coffee Joe Porter usually show up on tap at Atlantis before they do anywhere else.

A brightly lit bar by dive standards, the place is quite clean, and there's a rather large, rather well kept fish tank behind the bar … with actual living fish inside. The standard citywide beer and a shot (see Bob & Barbara's) can be had here for $3, though the beer served is Kenzinger. There's pool in back and a wide selection of board and card games. Atlantis gets packed on weekends, but has quite a few tables to accommodate the crowds. If you're late and can't grab one, just stand on the nicely polished wooden floor.

Nicely polished wooden floor? Great, craft beer selection? Brightly lit? Living fish in a clean tank? A dive? Well, while Atlantis isn't too dive-y on the inside, it definitely exhausts its dive qualities on the exterior. Add that to the fact that you wouldn't want to exactly walk home alone from the place and, yeah, dive it is.

Chug A Mug Pub

2301 E. Albert St.
Phone: 215-426-1105

Dive Bar Rating

On Sundays, there's always an RV parked outside of Chug A Mug. Throughout the day, patrons at the bar order a beer and a shot, down them, then head out front and get into the RV. Curious as to what the hell was going on, I questioned a man who was the stone opposite of sober. The man slurringly told me that, a few years back, the NFL Network decided to raise the price of its subscription rate for businesses. So, where you could've gotten something called the "Sunday Package" a season ago for X, now "they was chargin' Y to youse." In this story, Y was nearly quadruple the cost of X, a word this now very animated, drunken Fishtown lifer pronounced "kw-troo-peeled" over and over for emphasis. So, as a fuck you to the NFL Network and their "kw-troo-peeled" bourgeoisie rates, a regular of Chug's with an RV started parking out front every Sunday, patching into the cable line of the buildings out front and stealing the NFL Sunday Package.

On days when Chug A Mug isn't the site of felony cable theft, it's a dirt-cheap neighborhood bar adorned with a few grizzled veterans who've managed to so far survive the war they've waged against their own livers. They seem practically glued to their barstools, or, at the very least, that's the best possible explanation for what's keeping the wobbling sods from falling off them. Newcomers aren't warmly received, possibly because they're skittish about them pissing all over the NFL Network scam. Lots of Bud Lite is served here, mostly in bottles. It's available on tap too, but this isn't exactly the type of place where you can be certain that they're cleaning their draft lines with anything resembling regularity, so bottles are the safer choice.

Club Ozz

1155 N. Front St.
Phone: 215-203-7201

Dive Bar Rating

Club Ozz and its immediate surroundings are a location scout's dream ... if said location scout is looking for something described in the script as "a fresh slice of hell on earth, where dregs congregate and junkies cop."

Form a rectangle with your left index finger to your right thumb, and your right index finger to your left thumb, then look through it and scan the area around Club Ozz. You are directly underneath Philly's Blue Line, its Market-Frankford elevated train. It rumbles loudly above. A rat the size of a small poodle darts from behind a trashcan and heads into the sewer. Filet-o-fish wrappers from the McDonald's just up the block blow past like urban tumbleweeds. A fistfight breaks out between two men too drunk to connect any meaningful blows. There, in the middle of it all, sits Club Ozz, a sad strip club with a sign out front that looks like it was lifted from a print ad for shampoo in the '80s. Under the club name it reads "LAND OF MAKE BELIEVE FOR GENTLEMEN." Once inside, you'll wonder where these "gentlemen" are.

But first, a giant at the door will try to collect a cover charge from you. He will tell you, directly and with force, that it's $10. He can be talked down to $5. Should you really push it, he'll back down to nothing, his intimidating bark much louder than his bite. Once inside, you'll find a few lone men scattered around the bar, folded one-dollar bills in front of them. Young black women with ill-placed tattoos and some extra meat on their bones sit next to these men, occasionally getting up to sit in their laps to make small talk, and take off their bikini tops. The walls and bar are painted black. Stay long enough and you'll forget that sunlight exists. Color too, maybe, if it weren't for the bright red stage with two poles behind the bar.

Beers are relatively cheap for a strip club ($5 for a Yuengling), but more expensive than you'll find than at almost any of the dives within these pages. That includes Penns Port, where the women are much prettier and show off a lot more. To a soundtrack of Lil Wayne, Trick Daddy, Tevin Campbell and Petey Pablo (the latter's demands of "take your shirt off!" on "Raise Up" do not go unheeded here) a dancer at Ozz will come out and show off her wares on the large, boxy stage behind the bar, and twirl around one of the two poles on it. The men around the bar will then fling crumpled up dollar bills at the stage. Sometimes, if thrown with enough force, the bills will hit the dancer. No gentleman would ever do that.

Drew's Tavern

2401 E. Huntingdon St.
Phone: 215-423-3410

Dive Bar Rating

Drew's Tavern has been around for a long time, about fifty years, if the bartender here had to guess, though it has changed ownership and names frequently over the decades. The place's latest owner, Drew, bought it a few years back, and hasn't made many changes, save for a few flat screen TVs and some very fucking serious (and seriously contentious) pool tournaments held in the bar's back room, to which the bar's regulars bring their own screw-together pro-style sticks.

A Miller High Life will cost you $2.50, and there are special prices for takeout—24 ounce cans of Bud Ice will run you $1.75 or three for $5. The clientele of the bar is younger than at most dives, with twenty-something blue-collar men with closely cropped hair in hoodies excitedly watching Flyers and Eagles games and discussing the major plot points of the season finale of a show called *Sons of Anarchy*.

The walls of the place are beige, and the ceiling is made of tile. The oblong bar has ten or so stools around it, some of which are downright dangerous—lean on their backs with enough pressure and they'll fall right off, ensuing ball-busting calls for Drew to "replace these fuckin' things already." Dotted around the bar are several touch screen gambling games, an ATM and an Internet jukebox, which, it seems, is permanently stuck on Eminem.

Signs behind the bar convey the attitude of the place. There's one that says "I'm having a nice day, don't screw it up," and another that reads "I've stopped listening, why haven't you stopped talking?" If that doesn't convey the message, perhaps the photo of two regulars flipping off the camera will help make it clear. In other words, it's not too welcoming a spot. Still, the place does have its sweet side. Stay long enough, after the serious pool players, game watchers and *Sons of Anarchy* fans have stumbled home, and a regular is likely to bring his rescue Yorkshire Terrier, Rocky, into the bar. Rocky loves sniffing new people, and can hop from stool to unoccupied stool with astounding grace. He also loves to drink White Russians, and they'll let him up on the bar to have one if he's behaving.

El Bar

1356 N. Front St.
Phone: 215-634-6430

The sixth best thing about the El Bar is its back patio. Not only is it a refuge from the heavy smoke inside the place, but since the bar is located under the El Train (hence, the bar's name), when you're out on the patio, you feel like you're literally part of the train as it rumbles above. Even when you're relaxing with a cold one in one of the tiny plastic chairs in the glow of the Christmas lights that line the wall and fence and are strewn in the trees above, you still feel as if you are part of the hustle and bustle of the city.

The fifth best thing about the El Bar is *The Simpsons* pinball machine, truly one of the best pinball games ever made. The multi-ball on that thing is intense. And the pool table is pretty cool too.

The forth best thing about that El Bar is that it's a perfect hang that's never quite as crowded as Johnny Brenda's up the street.

The third best thing about El Bar is the "magic pizza" that shows up on the nights it does happen to get crowded. The bartender and owner just order it, and it appears, free for everyone in a gesture that'll warm the heart.

The second best thing about the El Bar is the $3 Citywide special—at El, a PBR pounder and a shot of Heaven Hill bourbon.

Finally, the best thing about the El Bar is the diverse lineup of live music that is crammed into the tiny, bare-brick backed stage—hip-hop, metal, jazz, and punk rock, plus a couple folk artists bring that bring in their acoustic guitars on open mike Wednesdays. And it's all free to boot.

Even if you choose to rank the El Bar's "bests" in a different order, there's a lot to like about the place.

NORTH PHILLY

PHILADELPHIA'S BEST DIVE BARS

El Cantinflas Bar & Tacos Place

110 W. Dauphin St.
No Phone

Dive Bar Rating

There is no better place In Philadelphia to watch a Phillies game than El Cantinflas Bar & Tacos Place in Kensington. That sounds like a bucket full of exaggeration, but I assure you it's not. Here's the proof: The Phillies are trailing the San Francisco Giants and wunderkind pitcher Tim Lincecum 4-1 in the ninth inning. After giving up a four pitch walk to the Flyin' Hawaiian, Shane Victorino, Lincecum is relieved by the Giant's closer, Brian Wilson. Despite the team's slim chances, somehow—maybe through taco osmosis or some weird third eye developed over copious shots of SoCo and Lime—the twenty-five or so Latinos at Cantinflas just know the Phillies are due for a comeback.

Then it happens. Chase Utley and Ryan Howard get on base. And when Jayson Werth, Lord of the Beard, hits a *jussst* fair double inside the right field line to clear the bases, Cantinflas erupts in hugs, dancing and more shots of SoCo and lime (the official drink of the place, or so it would seem.) The game goes into extra innings, eleven to be exact. No one is sitting, and every time anything of Phillies note happens, the folks at Cantinflas slap hard on their barstools. The Phillies take the lead, then give it away, then take it for good; the final score is 7 – 6. And you've never seen so many smiles or felt so much warmth.

This all takes place, mind you, without the benefit of announcers, as the TV is drowned out by blaring Latin music from a sound system that would make Susquehanna Bank Center (or whatever it's being called this week) envious. We're talking ear-rattling, deafness causing levels of music.

While inside Cantinflas it's festive, outside it's a bit sketchy. A block away from the El on the corner of N. Hope and E. Dauphin, two security cameras stand guard on both streets, their images shown on two TVs atop coolers behind the bar. Over the entrance to the bar is a warning about the cameras for those that might want to do the establishment or its patrons any harm: "ALL EYES ON YOU," it reads in bright red. Still, if you stay inside, and the Phillies win, you're guaranteed a good time—and many shots of SoCo and line. Just remember to bring earplugs. Oh, and someone who speaks Spanish, if only to get an explanation of the four giant Buddha statues behind the bar next to the Puerto Rican flags.

Era

2743 Fairmount
Phone: 215-769-7008

Dive Bar Rating

Era is a dive that, like Blue Nile Queen of Sheba II (see West Philly), also happens to serve up some damn good Ethiopian food. The place is located in the Fairmount neighborhood in the museum district, and a fair number of the bars and restaurants around it—London Grill, Bishops Collar, The Rose Tattoo—are pricey. Not Era, where a plate of food for two, which you eat with your hands, will run you $6, and bottles of Lager are $2 on Fridays and Saturdays. Shots of Heaven Hill Bourbon are always a buck.

Era opened in 2002. The walls are a dark wood, and three ceiling fans turn slowly above an oblong bar that's also constructed of sturdy, gorgeous wood. Behind the bar are handles of Captains and Seagram's, and what could be the world's largest bottle of Chambord, all stored cozily beneath a Commander 6300, those pesky alcohol shot regulators that insure that your bartender pours you a precise ounce every time and nothing more forever and ever amen. Era isn't the only place that uses the Commander or something like it—I've seen them at Five Points, Caprice Villa Lounge, Burg's Lounge and Queen of Sheba. At first I suspected that the reason for these was because ownership didn't trust its employees. But bartender Carolyn at Caprice says it's mostly to do with wily regulars who always demand a heavier pour. With the Commander 6300 or a similar shot regulator in place, the bartender has a built in excuse as to why they couldn't do a double pour, and tempers never flair much past annoyance because customers generally get it. So, the next time you peep a shot regulator, think of it less as a condom on the bottle inhibiting your liquid good times, and more of what it really is: a motherfucking live saver.

Fishtown's 15th Round

Dive Bar Rating

430 Belgrade St.
No Phone

Some of you may remember a YouTube series awhile back that featured three Fishtown curmudgeons critiquing modern music. It was called "Breakfast at Sulimay's" and it starred the pernicious Ann Bailey, the adorable Joe Walker and the mostly-quiet Bill Able, who would sit in a back booth in the venerable Fishtown diner Sulimay's while Marc Brodzik of Philadelphia's Scrapple TV pumped new hits into their ears via his laptop. Hearing the latest from artists they would never in a million years listen (or even be exposed) to—such as Animal Collective, Jay Reatard and Young Jeezy—the three of them would sit in judgment, *American Idol* style, the results of which usually inspired knee-slapping, gut-busting laughter. The series has been posted on popular music blogs and websites, and some of the videos have over 100,000 views, making the trio an online sensation.

I mention this because quiet Bill Able owns Fishtown's 15th Round. As a matter of fact, he owns the entire three story building the bar is housed in, so, when you walk into this well-lit ground-floor bar, you're essentially walking into his living room. Or at least it feels like that, because, right as rain and sure as shit, when you stumble through the front door, Bill Able will be sitting at the bar watching some sporting event on TV (boxing, most likely). Bill's a former boxer himself, as well as a lifetime resident of Fistown, and he is quick to complain about some of the visible changes taking place in the neighborhood, though he does it in a shoulder-shrugging "Whattya gonna do?" manner that's miles away from the similar but mean-spirited talk that takes place at joints like the Fishtown Tavern.

Bill uses the 15th Round like his own personal refrigerator, coming down during the day for a few 12-ounce curls, and generally parking on a barstool for good sometime around nightfall. Upstairs, he and his wife live on different schedules. And on different floors—she takes the second, he takes the third. He passes her on his way down for a beer, saying hello. "It sounds nuts," he says, a typical Bill smile cracking the edges of his mouth, "but that's the only way I've found to make a marriage work long term." Fishtowners of all generations and ages might agree on that one.

Fishtown Tavern

1301 Frankford Ave.
Phone: (215) 423-7220

A giant wooden sign carved to look like a fish hangs above the main entrance of the Fishtown Tavern, a tiny, smoke-filled room of mostly-regulars that, it's rumored, will shut its doors to customers should most of the regs already be inside. Why? Mainly because the Fishtown Tavern, more so than most of the dumps speckled throughout this mostly-Irish working class burg, is right in the crosshairs of the battle for the neighborhood's soul. You see, young, upwardly mobile kids are buying row homes in the neighborhood. These kids ride bikes. They read. They bring new businesses to the neighborhood. Most of those businesses are record stores and coffee shops. And the neighborhood lifers don't like this one bit.

The biggest fly in their old school ointment happens to be up the street from the Fishtown Tavern, a slick gastro-pub and live music venue called Johnny Brenda's. Named after an old boxer from the neighborhood, Fishtown lifers take exception to even the name of the place, complaining loudly and to anyone who will listen that the young punks watching their shitty indie rock, eating their mussels and drinking their pricey craft ales inside it don't even know who the hell Johnny Brenda (pronounced here as "Jorney Brender") was.

The conversation you overhear or participate in with the old heads here at the Fishtown Tavern is a microcosm of the culture war being fought not-so-quietly on the streets of the neighborhood. Many of the people within the smoky, smoky walls here talk about "what used to be" in ways that seem euphemistically racist. Or maybe they're just talking about the outrageous prices of the new places, as a bucket of 10 beers in this joint will run you $7.50. At those prices you'll be able to wash down plate after plate of whatever (hot dogs, pasta, changes nightly) it is gathering a potent wallop of gastrointestinal damage in the Sterno-heated chaffing dish in back by the pungent restrooms. Next to the food, sits a bottle of Scrubbing Bubbles, Tango air fresheners, and an old, open four pack of rusted D-batteries. Just the way Jorney Brender would've wanted it!

NORTH PHILLY

PHILADELPHIA'S BEST DIVE BARS

Gil's Goodtime Tavern

5956 Chester Ave.
Phone: 215-724-2500

Dive Bar Rating

I've heard it called both Gil's Goodtime Tavern and Good Times Bar, and, unfortunately, there aren't any signs out front to help. The bartender, when asked about this, has a question of her own. "You havin' a good time? Then it's a good time bar."

Either way, it's an odd name for a place to drink in after a funeral, but that's where a fella named Jim and his dressed-entirely-in-black crew have ended up, and not by mistake. "This is my bar," he says, a bit forlornly. "I drink here nearly everyday. Even today, when I buried my mother." Jim is a Fishtown lifer who, despite his grief (or perhaps because of it), doesn't mind telling the stranger next to him that he thinks his moustache makes him look "like a faggot… or a carnival worker." He then alternates between laughing and deep frowns, but stops just short of sobbing. His friends offer to buy him another shot, but he won't hear of it. Instead, the drinks are on him, and he's buying for everyone, even the faggot carnival worker with the moustache.

Running alongside the shotgun bar at Gil's is a shuffleboard bowling game called Master Strike. A man walks in and plops a duffle bag down on top of it. Inside the bag are a bunch of bootleg DVDs, which he's selling, one for $5, two for $9, three for $12. Jim looks through them, none-too-pleased with the selection, with Michael Jackson's *This Is It* earning his second homosexual slur of the night. Most of the movies he claims he's never heard of. "I'm gettin' old," he says after not being able to register *Julie and Julia*, *It's Complicated*, *Lovely Bones* or *Couples Retreat*. He settles on *The Blind Side* and *Public Enemies*. His drunk friends begin holding forth on the former, one insisting it's nothing but a chick flick, another saying it's the uplifting tale of triumph over adversity that Jim could use right now. I step in, saying, "Whatya think Jim is, some kind of faggot?" slip the entrepreneur with the duffle bag a five spot, grab *Public Enemies* from the stack and hand it to Jim. This is met with uproarious laughter from him and his friends. I'm now an honorary Fishtowner.

Smokiest Dives

Ray's Happy Birthday Bar

McGlinchey's

The Dive

12 Steps Down

Paddy's Old City Pub

Rosewood Bar

Friendly Lounge

Cookie's Tavern

Nickel Tavern

Half Time Good Time

120 Diamond
Phone: 215-425-7211

Dive Bar Rating

Say "the nice part of Kensington" to any Philadelphian who knows his ass from his elbow and they'll laugh right in your face, as the neighborhood is more known for gangs of Puerto Ricans driving noisy dirt bikes and mini race wars than anything nice. But lo and behold, on the corner of Diamond and Howard, right across from cutesy Norris Square, sits Half Time Good Time, a nice Kenzo sports bar with a picturesque view of the nice green patch of earth across the street.

Despite it being nice and all, there are a few weird things about Half Time Good Time. First, everyone calls it "Good Time Bar," but lest you confuse it with Gil's Good Time Tavern (also sometimes called "Good Time Bar") in nearby Fishtown, I'll call it by its official name here. Second, there is no real sports identity at Half Time. Where most Philadelphia sports bars are shrines to Philly teams and heroes, Half Time seems to celebrate teams and individuals with no rhyme or reason. Thus, there are five Wheaties boxes atop a take out cooler (stocked with to-go forties), most of them celebrating various Yankee's World Series victories. (One box has a picture of Joe Torre on it). Another box of Kellogg's Corn Flakes proudly displays a member of the Pittsburgh Pirates who I don't recognize because, really, who recognizes anyone from the Pirates? Beside the cereal boxes are posters of Cal Ripken, along with one of his framed batter's gloves, signed and with a certificate of authenticity.

The wall behind the barstools is a museum to boxing greats, Philadelphian and otherwise. Bernard Hopkins (Philly!) posters sit alongside promotional signage for the epic Ali vs. Frazier (Philly!) fights from days of yore. Lots of signed pictures of Roberto Duran hang on the walls, and one wonders if this is in celebration of one of the greatest boxing careers ever, or a bar in a mostly-Puerto Rican neighborhood reminding their Panamanian brothers of the man who quit so publicly in his fight against Sugar Ray Leonard.

In the back of the place, an Eagles themed football field is painted on the ceiling above a pool table. Lots of large basketball sneakers are tied to a pole at the end of the bar, and still more signed basketballs, footballs and baseballs stay concealed behind Plexiglas. Beside all the memorabilia is a New York Giants football helmet? The fuck? Like "the nice part of Kensington," Half Time is a conundrum. After a few $2 Lagers I make like Duran: "No mas."

Best Karaoke Dives

Ray's Happy Birthday Bar

Bob & Barbara's

Queen of Sheba

12 Steps Down

Abby's Desert Lounge

J.R.'s Saloon

Westy's Tavern

Jack's Famous Bar

853 E. Allegheny Ave.
Phone: 215-634-6616

Dive Bar Rating

There was a time, back in the middle of the twentieth century, when Kensington was one of America's busiest manufacturing areas, filled with mills, dye factories and other bustling textile-related businesses that gainfully employed thousands of workers. The block of Kensington and Allegheny, or K&A as it's called by its residents, was a particularly white-hot hub, a "marketplace perpetually teeming with commuters and shoppers," wrote *Philly Weekly* scribe F.H. Rubino in an article about Ken Milano's book about the neighborhood, *The History of the Kensington Soup Society*. Those high times are in heady contrast to the stark reality facing the neighborhood today, which finds burnout junkies scratching violently at their skin, prostitutes working the track, and general shiftiness at every turn.

Enter Jack's Famous Bar, one of the greatest dive bars in the city, if not the country. The place has been owned and operated by brothers Mel and Joe Adelman since the early '60s. Their father Al bought the bar in 1945 from the titular Jack, and the family never bothered changing the name. It's not the only thing that hasn't changed. Food and drink can be had here for so little, you wonder how they can turn a profit: 45 cents for a tub of potato salad; $1.75 for a liverwurst and onions sandwich; the same for a draft pint. Of course, if you want to bring in your own food, that's fine too, though they'll charge you a dollar for the luxury.

The main attraction at Jack's, though, isn't the rock bottom booze prices, but the booze itself, as behind the bar, stacked on shelves that reach the ceiling, are 400 bottles of oh-so-very old whiskey and other brown spirits from way back when the original Jack owned the joint. As Mel explains it, back then spirits had to be bought in bulk, as there was a liquor quota. The extra bottles were put up on the wall, and those bottles remain there today, unopened and full of various brown liquors that have been there for some seventy years, some from before World War II. The bottles are covered in dust, and Mel says they tried to clean them, but when they did, the old labels got wiped off the bottles. So, he'd rather leave well enough alone. For the sake of ambience and history, you'll be glad he did.

Jerry's Bar

129 Laurel St.
Phone: 610-623-9091

Dive Bar Rating

Once a Slavic working class burg, Northern Liberties has changed quite a bit over the past decade. It now has boutique shops, nice restaurants, a classy beer outlet called The Foodery, a bowling alley with glow in the dark lanes equipped to tell you the speed of the ball you just rolled, "green" condos and a skate shop. And, you can actually park your car on its streets these days without fear that your windows will be smashed.

The hub of the "new" Northern Liberties is the Piazza at Schmidts (built in and around the old Schmidts brewery), the brainchild of developer Bart Blanstein, who says he built the thing instead of buying a fancy sports car as a reaction to his midlife crisis. Must've been some crisis: the development features an 80,000 square foot open-air plaza, 35 artist studios and boutiques, four restaurants, 500 apartments and 50,000 square feet of office space, fulfilling Blatstein's dream of creating a "five minute neighborhood" where people can "live, shop, eat, work and play, all within a few city blocks."

In stark contrast to the Piazza sits Jerry's, which has hugged its tiny corner close to I-95 since the early '70s. In fact, when they were building the freeway, workers used to lower their ladders into Jerry's from the overpass, climb down, and get food. Jerry's is one of the last remaining Slavic businesses in the area (R.U.B.A. Hall and Pernitsky's Bar being the others). Owner Jaroslaw "Jerry" Lebin lives above the bar, and on most days can be found sitting at it. He is truly one of the sweetest old guy's you'll ever meet, happy to talk to strangers or leave them be. On the walls around the place are worn photos of his parents (his father owned the bar before him), the soccer teams he's coached over the years, a map of the Ukraine and a sticker that reads "The Navy Yard is ... Americans working for America." Behind the bar you'll find the usual big domestic beers and a few off the beaten path varieties, like Obolon, a Ukrainian lager. Unlike most Philly spots, Jerry's doesn't have any daily or happy hour specials, as Jerry doesn't see the need. "Everyday here is a special," he says. "Our prices are low." Most drafts and bottles will run you two and a quarter. Smoking is allowed—and preferred.

J.R.'s Saloon

2663 E. Norris St.
No Phone

Dive Bar Rating

Jim Rowson, owner of J.R.'s Saloon in Fishtown, and I have some history. Back in March of 2008, *Philadelphia Weekly* put out a Top 50 Bars issue. The list was flawless and indisputable. Unfortunately, many readers didn't feel the same way. One of those readers was Jim. He wrote in, and said he'd like to take us on a Fishtown dive crawl, to visit some real dive bars, if anyone was interested. I called him, and off we went.

Jim's a nice guy, if a bit eccentric. He's got tattoos on each arm. The left has the names of women he's dated over the years. They're all crossed out, except for his wife's. The tattoo on his right arm is faded, and features a duck carrying a hypodermic needle. During the course of our crawl, he took me to six or seven places, the last spot being his own. Along the way he introduced me to some of the bars you'll find in this book, real blue-collar bars that have been around for generations, places that, according to Jim, smell like ass and bleach. The former, he explained, was because the clientele of these joints is made up of mostly sweaty men fresh off their manual labor jobs. The latter is to combat the former.

Jim prides himself on carrying the most single malt Scotch in the entire city at his place, a no frills joint that hugs I-95 and opens at 7 a.m. for its regulars, known as the Breakfast Club, who come in every morning after working the night shift. Whether he carries the most I cannot say for sure, but I do know that no one can compete with the prices of the stuff he does stock. A glass of hard-to-come-by Redbreast Irish whiskey, for instance, will cost you $6 at J.R.'s. By comparison, it will run you $21 at Iron Chef Jose Garces' posh Village Whiskey. And remember, at J.R.'s you can sip your Redbreast at seven in the morning, while playing a game of pool.

Krupa's Tavern

2701 Brown St.
Phone: 215-765-7769

Dive Bar Rating

Next time you visit your grandparents, go into the bathroom, open their medicine cabinet, and check out all the pills they take. There's one for creaky bones, ACE Inhibitors for blood pressure, a blood thinner, another for something you never knew existed, etc. In all, dozens of pills, taken every day, so many that they have to use little dispensers marked with the day of the week to keep track of them all. Lined up next to one another, the bottles seem to go on forever. This will one day be your life.

There can be no doubt that getting old sucks. Your skin wrinkles, your hair goes white, your hearing says adios (only you won't hear it), your vision says bye-bye, and you're cold all the time. In exchange, you get wisdom. A sad tradeoff, it seems to me. However, let me let you in on a little secret that will help you to cope with your fade into the *Cocoon* years: Go to Krupa's Tavern in Fairmount.

Tiny, always quiet, there is something about Krupa's that has a way of soothing the soul. Here the world seems to stop, the hustle and bustle of your daily life pointless in the face of Krupa's old men bartenders and the large mirror behind the bar. Those old men bartenders have been at Krupa's since Rocky first ran the steps at the Philadelphia Museum of Art just a few blocks away, and are more interested in watching the college football, basketball or Phillies game they have playing on the tube (at a reasonable volume) than they are in making meaningless chit chat with you. And, if they did chat with you, it would inevitably be about whatever game was on the tube anyway. This doesn't come across as unfriendly. Instead, it's peaceful, and somehow makes the prospect of getting old a little more palatable.

Smoking is no longer permitted here, but the air is still stale from the decades when it was. That stale air is a good thing, it turns out, as it's the only reason you won't spend all day inside, sipping your suds quietly, listening to the low hum of sports, contemplating life and death.

Now, remove yourself from that stool, go out and get some fresh air. Then run those museum steps just to prove to the world that you can, old man.

Les-N-Doreen's Happy Tap

Dive Bar Rating

1301 E. Susquehanna Ave.
Phone: 215-634-1123

A neighborhood bar in every sense—equally fabulous and depressing—L&D is also a mirror reflecting old school Fishtown back onto itself. Like an ongoing casting call for *What Not To Wear*, the hallowed hall of L&D is a never ending parade of Silver Tab jeans, Teva sandals with black socks, denim shorts warn below the knee, and many more crimes against good taste. Tim Gunn would have a heart attack if he visited this place.

Good thing then that Les-N-Doreen's has plenty of dirt-cheap beer and booze to quiet Gunn's pulse. Pints of Lager and High Life are a measly $1.50, and the good-natured bartenders will refill your glass even if you haven't asked them to. It's no wonder then the barstools are usually teeming with regulars, all of whom bask in the cheap prices and fact that they can light up here. Like a lot of Fishtown joints, Les-N-Doreen's is proudly Irish; a small Leprechaun is pictured on the sign out front and lots of them are painted behind the bar. Look closely and you'll wonder how drunk the person painting them was, as they all have pretty girlish faces with thick, reddish-brown beards, the cutest little cross-dressing Leprechauns you'll ever see.

The ceiling is blotched with green paint for a sponge-patted effect that makes it look as if a group of those Leprechauns threw up in the absence of gravity. Secondhand smoke and tar from decades of smoking cakes the areas in between their upchuck. Hand written signs taped to the mirror behind the bar offer specials and new products. One of them is the sickeningly sweet Choco Vine, a red wine and chocolate mixture that they'll sell you in a shot for $3 or over ice for $5. Before you order either version, know this: It starts like Kahlua, and finishes with the faint taste of earwax.

Inexplicably and to no ones benefit, Les-N-Doreen's sometimes employees a DJ. She sits at a table in back, blocking the men's restroom with her laptop, and plays horrific dance remixes of old Elvis and James Brown classics at top volume. At other times, the place is near silent, the only soundtrack either provided by the Phillies game or local news being broadcast on all three TVs, or the sound of old men coughing up phlegm between drags.

Little Station

Station 2974 Aramingo Ave.
(corner of Aramingo Ave. and Ann St.)

Dive Bar Rating

Little Station in Port Richmond is a weird little joint. While it might be more accurate to call it a takeout spot than a bar, it's got a bar too. A very dive-y bar, as a matter of fact. So in this book it goes.

The ratty little building on Aramingo and Ann that it's located in is split in half. The front part is a bar, the back a beer takeout/ storage spot where old Asian ladies sit behind protective Plexiglas. (The front door bar entrance is locked, so those who choose to enter the place are forced to use the back entrance where the beer storage is.) The front bar area isn't behind Plexiglas, which makes the use of it in back confusing. Only "bar" isn't exactly right, I suppose. Basically, if you have nowhere to go or no one to go home to, Little Station offers five stools where you're allowed to sit and drink beer you just bought from the coolers in back. However, not many folks seem to want stick around the dingy digs. On the night I was there, the only people in the place where two old men sharing a six pack of Bud tall boys, smoking and playing cards. They told me they like coming here because it's quiet, and that it also lets them get away from their wives.

There is no ambience or décor to speak of. The walls are unadorned faux wood. There are cages on the front door and on the one leading to the take out in back. The front bar area is mostly used for storing cases and cases of beer that can't fit in the cooler. Drink a beer up front and you'll see dozens of men and women, young and old, of all races, coming in to buy forties of Old English or six packs of High Life. Most of them jet back right out of the place after copping their goods. To be honest, Little Station doesn't really give them a reason stay.

Luke's Bar

2434 Cedar St.
Phone: 215-634-2106

Dive Bar Rating

At night, Luke's Bar has one of the coolest signs in Philadelphia. While there's nothing fancy about it—it's just a rectangle with the bar's name on it—built inside are tiny blinking, colored lights that flicker, burst and hum. It seems like the spirits of the dead power those lights. More specifically, one dead spirit, as according to the bar's regulars, Luke's is haunted by its recently deceased, eponymous owner, Luke McGahan, who died of a stroke in early '08. Whether or not his spirit still lingers inside his bar is up for debate. Fond memories of him, however, definitely still haunt the place.

All around Luke's, there is plenty for its old, dearly departed namesake to do, as the place is jam-packed with trinkets and doodads. There's a video poker game, a pool table, a piano, components for Rock Band that are hooked up to a giant TV in back that everyone seems to ignore, a few classy velvet paintings, and tons of unframed photographs pinned up on the walls. No matter where Luke is spending eternity, he'll spend a good deal of it trying to get through all those photos.

In November 2009, Luke's celebrated its 40th anniversary, earning it the title of "Oldest Bar in Fishtown with the same owner," according to Luke's widow, Terry Burns-McGahan. Many of the folks here are regulars who enjoy sitting around the J-shaped bar puffing on their cigarettes and drinking their tiny ponies of Bud or Bud Lite from a bucket filled with ice. A bucket of 10 will run you roughly $7. Physically, the place is broken up into two rooms. The front houses the bar and Rock Band, while in the back are the pool table and piano. There's a fairly large cutout window behind the bar that allows you to keep tabs of who is racking them up or tickling the ivories. If you're lucky, someone will fill the bar with some piano playing. One of the nights I was here, a guy starting playing a not-terrible version of the Beatles "Strawberry Fields." When he finished, he was greeted by applause from a few patrons at the bar. "One of Luke's favorites," one of them said, an undeniable longing in her eyes. "One of Luke's favorites."

Melrose Bar

635 W. Girard Ave.
No Phone

Dive Bar Rating

Bartender Diane says that the Melrose Bar isn't as busy as it used to be. And she should know, as she's been here, popping cans of Old English and twisting caps of Colt 45, for just over ten years, just under half the time that the Melrose has been open. She blames the "meters"—the electronic pouring system that measures shots exactly and without prejudice—that the owner installed about two years ago for the decline in business, "People know they'll never get extra," she deadpans. "They don't like that."

Diane has been married for 19 years, and been with the same man for almost 30. They lived together for ten years before they made it official because, she says, that's how long it takes to get to know someone. The characters on *Maury*, to which she's offering color commentary, never got to know one another, having only been together for three years before they got hitched. That's why Quentin is about to tell his wife about the sex tape he made with her best friend. Each new twist in the story is met with an "Oh, Lord," "Oh, God" or "Oh, Jesus" from Diane, who sucks on gummy worms and buzzes in the occasional customer at the door.

The Melrose Bar is on bustling Girard Avenue, on the corner of 7th, next to an abandoned lot. It's a long shotgun bar with unadorned walls that are painted a boring beige. A row of old deli tables is lined up against the opposite side of the bar. They sell a couple varieties of chips for snacks, but nothing else food-wise. Smoking isn't allowed here, and Diane is glad for that, she says, adjusting the gold stud in her nose. During the commercial break, she waxes nostalgic about the right way to raise kids. Hers are 31 and 28, respectively. They're out of her way now, thank God, and no longer require much. They still call her often with their troubles, and when they do she takes the time to listen. "Because that's what they really want. They just want you to listen. Even when they ask for advice, they don't want it—just want you to listen to their problem," she says, sucking on another sour worm. "I learned some of that at this job," she says before adding another "Oh, Lord."

Old Philadelphia Bar

2118 E. Dauphin St.
No Phone

Dive Bar Rating

The first time I went to the Old Philadelphia Bar, I was given two bits of advice: Don't go at night, and don't order anything on tap. The reason for the first is obvious, as, according to my source, a Fishtown lifer, nighttime ain't the right time in the neighborhood where the bar is located. Go there after sundown, he told me, and the chances are you're going to get mugged or beaten. As for the taps, he told me that they don't clean their lines.

In reality, the tap thing is a stupid myth, according to the bar's owners, who insist that they clean their lines every Thursday. As for not going at night, that seems a tad bit overstated too, as nothing you'll see outside of OPB seems even vaguely threatening once you've been to, say, Billy's Chili Pot or Cousin Danny's Exotic Haven.

Once inside the Old Philly Bar, night or day, the prices are dirt cheap. You can purchase three seven-ounce chilled mugs of beer for $1.75, a pint for $1.35 and a 24-ounce can of Bud Ice for $1.50. At these prices, you can reasonably drink yourself into a coma for cheaper than you would be able to at home. Hell, beer here is cheaper than a bottle of water, and it's a wonder more people aren't inside OPB day and night, clean lines or dirty, sucking down suds.

That isn't to say the place isn't crowded. It is, at all hours. And beer isn't the only bit of booze they sell, as they have a bar better stocked with the hard stuff than some Atlantic City casinos. If they've got one bottle of Jack Daniels or Jim Beam, OPB has fifteen, stacked deep and in impressive, mesmerizing rows. The sheer volume of liquor for such a not-all-that-huge place speaks to how much the average customer here is putting away.

The bar itself is shaped like a rectangle, allowing maximum efficiency when ordering. By virtue of its shape, you'll often find yourself directly facing someone on the other side of the bar. If you're lucky, like I was, you'll get to see a rail-thin white man make out with a 300 plus pound black woman, both missing a few teeth. My Fishtown friend who recommended the OPB took this outburst of alcohol-fueled tonsil hockey and groping as a sign of how the neighborhood has changed for the better. "Five years ago, they wouldn't have gotten out of there alive," he told me. But they do. And when I leave the bar, the lovely couple, a shining beacon of Fishtown progress, are snorting cocaine off the dashboard of a car parked right out front.

OMAC

Front & Norris
No Phone

Dive Bar Rating

OMAC is the acronym for One Man Army Corps, and a large piece of art displaying a dozen or so of the DC Comics that the bar is named after hang on the wall when you enter. O-Mac also happens to be the nickname of the bar's owner, a friendly guy who, much to the delight of anyone with a pulse and sense of humor, will drop his own money in the Touch Tunes juke to put on R. Kelly's wonderfully comic "Real Talk," which he'll then sing along to between sips of the Everfresh Premium cranberry juice and vodka he keeps behind the bar with him in a tiny plastic cup.

O-Mac is also soused or insensitive enough to show the regulars at the bar camera phone pictures of the girl he took out the night before. She pissed herself, he says, and photos of her humiliation delight the regulars here who, despite her unfortunate first-date accident, tell O she's "pretty enough to give another shot." O-Mac agrees. Lord knows, he's been that drunk before too.

In two coolers behind the bar, 40-ounce bottles of Silver Thunder are sold for $2.50. Pints of anything during happy hour are a dollar cheaper still. Those coolers are kept running by some of the most precarious wiring you'll likely ever see. They practically scream fire hazard. One of the coolers even has a partially exposed fan at the bottom, just begging to take the toes off of someone who has had a bit too much. On top of the coolers are cases of Herr's chips. Visible behind the bar are a bottle of hot sauce, a bottle of rubbing alcohol and a tiny bucket of Olympic paint. The paint is there because O-Mac is renovating his joint. As a result of the renovations in progress, there's a pool table in back that can't be used at the moment, and the restroom is currently unisex, as O-Mac has started, but hasn't finished, work on the ladies' room. In the men's room hangs a framed poster/wall calendar from a Gentleman's club, Club Risque, and two mostly-naked and partially moist women watch over you as you pee. Over one of the women is written the following: "To O-Mac, Can't wait to suck that big dick of yours! MMMM heart, Jaguar."

Good Food

Cherry Street Tavern

Midtown II

CoCo's

Oscar's

Las Vegas Lounge

Era

Abyssinia (below Fiume)

Pen & Pencil

Locust Rendezvous

McGillin's Olde Ale House

R.U.B.A. Hall

414 Green St.
Phone: 215-627-9831

Dive Bar Rating

The name stands for Russian United Beneficial Association (not Russian Ukranian Boating Association, as many think) and it traces its history back to 1914, when it opened as a meeting place for the then-healthy Northern Liberties Slavic population to address the concerns of their neighborhood and socialize. After prohibition ended, they wisely added alcohol. These days, although the neighborhood has changed dramatically, its Russian population reduced drastically, membership from old Slavs remains relatively strong despite the fact that the bar was bought by a new owner in March of 2010.

There was a lot of fear from the community when the sale went down, in particular, fear that the character of the bar would change. Fortunately, these fears turned out to be unfounded, as the new ownership has kept the place the same, save for a foray into the arts. As a result, on any given night on the tiny downstairs stage, you might see a screening of a film made by a local, a live band, standup comedy, burlesque or a variety show. Upstairs, the famous ballroom plays host to all sorts of events as well—birthday parties, wedding anniversaries, children's christenings. In many ways, the place incorporates the community more than ever. The new ownership has even kept the place "members only," and while that membership may have jumped from $5 to $20, the fact that it remains is a nod to R.U.B.A.'s days of yore.

Also a nod: the look of the place. There are a couple mounted deer heads along the walls, and the hand painted ceiling beams feature child-like murals of beach scenes and milk maids. Smoking is still allowed (in fact, there are still ashtrays mounted on the restroom walls). Behind the bar are all types of knick-knacks: a tiny bust of Elvis, a snare drum, two accordions, one of those cymbal crashing monkey dolls and a host of other curios. Also remaining in place are the bar's gorgeous frescoed ceiling, lantern light fixtures and dark wood bar. There's also a free pool table, Foozball and darts, but the highlight of the room has to be a painting of three women at the shore wearing bikinis. When the new owner bought the place, he replaced some of the sheetrock upstairs that had been in disrepair. Behind one of the walls was this painting, which had apparently been done sometime in the 1960s. It looks as though it could've been hanging in Dean Martin's living room. Come to think of it, R.U.B.A. kinda looks like Dean Martin's living room itself.

Best Pickup Spots

Locust Bar

McGlinchey's

Oscar's

Bob & Barbara's

The Dive

Side Street Café

2300 E. Venango St.
No Phone

Dive Bar Rating

The name "Side Street Café" evokes a classy, hidden gem of a place, maybe in Tuscany or Rome, where people dine alfresco under the stars, pouring Chianti freely from wicker covered bottles that sit on red-and-white checkered tablecloths next to breadbaskets filled with rosemary-rubbed focaccia. While this Side Street Café definitely ain't *that* place, it is still a gem of sorts.

The tiny, box-shaped bar is painted pea-soup green, and wears its Irish heritage proudly on its puke-flecked sleeve. The distinct smell of body odor and disinfectant wafts mightily in the air, to the point where, upon entering, you may gag a little. Hardened Fishtown lifers with bad teeth and worse livers dot the bar, and occasionally, if one of them feels the urge, a round will be bought for everyone sitting around it. The bartender places tiny plastic cough medicine cups in front of everyone to mark the good will gesture. You can trade the cup for a bottle of beer or ask the bartender to fill it with something from the bottom shelf, the only shelf you'll find at Side Street.

If it's anytime close to St. Patrick's Day (a holiday that generally seems to last half the year here), the patrons will be in an especially giving mood. Their generosity should be matched by some of your own, because it's rude not to buy should you choose to accept. (And, you have no choice but to accept.) There's a cigarette machine on the back wall that, I'm told by a regular, used to sell a pack for 33 cents. "You'd put 35 cents in the machine and a pack would come out with two cents taped to it!" The Side Street has two volumes, it seems, eerie silence or deafening jukebox overkill, often times Led Zeppelin or the Stones.

And now, a joke from a drunken customer: His Holiness the Pope is scheduled to visit New York City. But he has a dilemma. Because His Holiness the Pope travels in a carpool, you see, and the only way to get into the city is through the Holland or Lincoln Tunnels. And this is a problem, you see, because His Holiness the Pope has "carpool tunnel syndrome." This joke is followed with silence, and then a giant, building-shaking burp from the guy who told it.

Tailgators Sports Bar

2436 Gaul St.
No Phone

Dive Bar Rating

Can you remember back to a time when Mel Gibson wasn't a bat shit crazy anti-Semite who'd left his wife of a bazillion years for a young piece of model-hot strangeness he would go on to physically, mentally and verbally abuse? When, instead of his movies being vehicles for his own nihilistic blood thirst, they were, y'know, entertaining? Movies like *Lethal Weapon*, all four of them, *The Year of Living Dangerously*, *Mad Max* and *Maverick*! Remember *Maverick*?

So what happened to Mel? Not being a trained psychiatrist, I don't know, but what I do know is that Tailgators (terrible name, fun bar) has a fucking *Maverick* pinball machine in it! That's pretty damn thrilling. Who even knew they existed? After enough cheap booze and specialty shots (I had no idea what impossibly sweet fruity things I was drinking, and the bartender was no help) every game of *Maverick* features multi-ball.

Physically, Tailgators is a pretty non-descript joint. There's plain beige/orange-tinged wood all around the interior and the place seems to be more of a takeout bar for sixers or 40s than a place that anyone actually stays at and drinks in. I was told by a local, however, that "the bartender's huge titties are always hanging out," and that that offers incentive for people to drink in-house. However, if you decide to drink here, be sure to limit your intake to alcohol, because the bar failed a health inspection in 2009 for, among other things, storing food too closely to the floor, and not hanging a broom properly. Also, the bartender with the hanging-out titties isn't food safety certified. So don't eat at Tailgators. Just come for ol' *Maverick*, and consider Mel's descent into madness. Then do a few sweet shots and consider your own.

Tony's Way

Front & Berks
Phone: 215-423-3033

Dive Bar Rating

A second room to the right of the entrance at Tony's has a pool table, and through the entryway leading to it is a sign that reads "Complaint Department: Please Take a Number." The kicker is that the numbers are attached to the pin of a grenade.

Though that may suggest that Tony's is not a particularly friendly place, in truth it just shows that they're not interested in bullshit, racial or otherwise. The bar is on the Fishtown cusp, but its patronage is mostly made up of Puerto Ricans from nearby Port Richmond and Kensington. Owner Anthony "Tony" Santiago Jr. is himself Puerto Rican, but that matters little. "This bar is strictly welcoming to everyone," he told *Philadelphia Weekly* in June of '09 in regards to the racial makeup of his bar and the neighborhood. He doesn't tolerate intolerance. "I don't play that shit. When people say something stupid we correct them right away. I'll throw you out myself, physically."

Tony was a member of the highway patrol for twenty-seven years, before becoming then-mayor Ed Rendell's driver and bodyguard. Through his job with Rendell, he met lots of celebs, and is happy to tell you about them: Angie Dickinson, Harry Belafonte, Gregory Peck. Through his job with the force, however, he also earned a bit of heartache, which he will also tell you about: his partner was gunned down while off-duty one Christmas Eve while trying to break up a fight at a bar.

Bottles of beer during happy hour are a buck fiddy, and they'll serve them to you with a smile. Around the oblong bar in the center of Tony's, men sit and drain their pints one slow sip at a time, none of them in any kind of rush. Though there's a Touch Tunes jukebox, no one drops any money in it, so the place is quiet much of the time. (Except when the El train rumbles by, as the bar sits in the shadow of the El train's Berk Station on the corner of Front and Berks.) Quiet enough, in fact, that if you do say some "stupid shit" Tony will definitely hear it. And when he does, you'll be dusting yourself off underneath the El.

Westy's Tavern

1440 Callowhill St.
Phone: 215-563-6134

Dive Bar Rating

Also known as "Westy's on 15th" or just plain "Westy's" to its regulars, this no-frills, straight forward, Irish-tinged bar is located right across the street from the iconic and historic building that houses both of Philadelphia's daily newspapers, the *Inquirer* and the *Daily News*. As such, it's a newspaperman's bar. Thus, you'll often find beat reporters, columnists and the like cozying up to the bar. Even in their absence, their presence remains in a sign hanging over the bar that reads, "Sorry … yesterday was the deadline for all complaints." Alongside these men telling their war stories of a dying industry are sports fans taking in games on Westy's primo sound system and flat screens, as well as burnouts hanging out in this virtual no man's land stretch of neighborhood just north of City Hall and right next to highway 76. It's an interesting mix to say the least.

Westy's is currently in the process of a hefty renovation that promises a new floor, live entertainment, a menu overhaul and outdoor speakers. They speculate that it'll all be done by the time this book hits shelves. Still, even with a sleeker look, its character as a solid spot to sip a fairly large variety of suds—dive-tastic standards like PBR, Bud and Miller and more well-to-do choices like Woodchuck Cider, Stella, Victory and Harp—with one of the city's most diverse clientele should remain.

At night, the crowd gets considerably younger, particularly on Thursday and Saturday, when DJ Jack Keenan brings his karaoke machine to the party. On these nights you can add a $5 bucket of pretty damn aiiight wings (a crowd favorite that will remain after the menu switch) to the $3 sixteen ounce cans of Rolling Rock that are available all day every day. While the karaoke crowd can swell at times, there's also plenty else to do around the joint, such as looking in the mirrors hung alongside the bar that have pictures of Philadelphia catch-alls like Rocky, the Liberty Bell and the Art Museum painted on them. Or you make a phone call on the actual working pay phone by the exit. Don't laugh—some of those old-timer newspapermen wouldn't know a smart phone if it put them out of a job.

Yesterday's Tavern

2448 E. Huntingdon St.
Phone: 215-634-6464

Located in a part of Fishtown that seems to have a bar on every corner, what makes Yesterday's Tavern worth a visit are the loyal customers. While the current owners have only had the keys for seven years, many of their customers have been coming in for thirty plus, back when the place was called Erin's, and before that when it was called Meg's. The prices are still cheap, and they know their friends will be here, even if the sign out front has changed. It's just a big ole sloppy Fishtown love affair, and even as an outsider, it is fun to be part of. The locals come in to play darts, and complain that they "haven't been able to hit that Goddamn 19 all Goddamn night." They also play air drums wildly and without fear of being judged. At the end of the night, they know they can walk out with a six-pack of cold Bud cans to go for $7.50. They sing-along loudly to whatever's coming out of the digital juke, a surprising mix of Oasis and Coldplay for a crowd whose average age is … well, let's just say no one at Yesterday's has been asked for their ID in some time.

Around an oddly shaped, not-quite horseshoe bar are fifteen or so stools. The walls are the color of ketchup and mustard mixed together, and on them hang pictures of an incongruous assortment of different music and Hollywood stars. There's a poster from the original Sinatra version of *Ocean's 11*. Jackie Gleason smiles from a picture of him dressed as Ralph Kramden. There are also photos of a shirtless Jim Morrison, The Beatles and Bill Haley & the Comets. The biggest picture of them all, though, is of Robert Redford and Paul Newman in a still from *Butch Cassidy and the Sundance Kid*. If either one of those sharpshooters were here, you can rest assured they'd hit that Goddamn 19.

Hide-A-Way Inn

WEST PHILLY

Abby's Desert Lounge

4704 Baltimore Ave.
Phone: 215-727-4560

Dive Bar Rating

The sign out front of Abby's Desert Lounge features a camel standing beneath a couple of desert palms. The desert theme stops with the bar's name and sign, however, though the place really is a sweet West Philly oasis.

Located on a fabulously diverse chunk of newly rejuvenated Baltimore Avenue, Abby's is right next door to Dahlak, an Ethiopian restaurant that, like Gojjo and Queen of Sheba down the street, have turned Baltimore Avenue into what Penn University's paper *The Daily Pennsylvanian* has dubbed "a vegan Mecca." Around the corner, the friendly Fu-Wah Mini Market makes the best tofu banh mi on the planet, while its sister restaurant, Vietnam, serves up out-of-this-world Vietnamese noodle dishes, spring rolls and quite a bit more from their seemingly endless menu. There's also a yoga studio a short hop down, and the Danger Danger House a block away on 47th—a gigantic Victorian home housing crust punks, musicians and artists of every ilk, which used to put on some truly bizarre and headline making basement punk rock shows. All of this is plunked down in a neighborhood in West Philly, Cedar Park, that's 90 percent African American, according to the 2000 census.

Unsurprisingly, then, Abby's is a black-owned bar with a mostly black clientele, though it has welcomed the diversity of the neighborhood with open arms. On any given night, your barstool neighbor may be a white kid with dreads in serious need of a bath, some well dressed Penn kids going deeper into West Philly than their RA back at the dorm ever recommended or, most likely, a middle-aged or old black man or woman talking about how their beloved Cedar Park has changed, but with less suspicion and fear about the inevitable gentrification at their doorstep than other neighborhood bars undergoing similar fates.

Abby's is tiny—a shotgun bar that's usually quite full, hugging white brick walls. Moving around can be difficult. The bartenders are relatively jovial, and often sing with or dance to whatever music is playing. On Fridays, the place plays host to live music, usually R&B, but occasionally they'll book a hip-hop act from the neighborhood. Fridays, understandably, are packed.

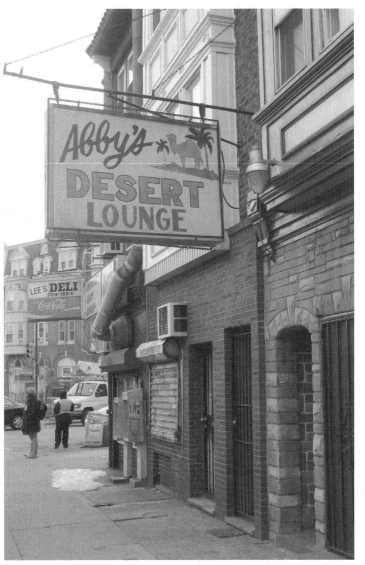

Billies Boomer Lounge

227 S. 52nd St.
No Phone

One of Barack Obama's last campaign stops before his historic 2008 election was in the predominantly black neighborhood of West Philly. Obama spoke from an elaborate stage set up on the corner of 52nd and Locust, in front of thousands upon thousands. Billies Boomer Lounge was his unlikely backdrop.

The Obama Team's choice of locale that day wasn't random. Up and down 52nd, sometimes called "the strip" or "West Philly's Main Street," burned out and boarded up abandoned shells of businesses are ubiquitous. While trash is a problem everywhere in the city, on 52nd it blows around in the wind in tiny garbage tornados, blanketing the street. The corner of 52nd and Market had the dubious distinction of being named one of Philly's "Top 10 Drug Corners" in a 2007 story by *Philadelphia Weekly*. The area's poverty level is 19.1 percent, according to the 2000 census. Since the bottom fell out of the economy, it's reasonable to assume that's edged up a bit. Thus, Obama's message of "change" would have particular resonance here.

Billies Boomer sits quietly in the middle of it all. The bar's white brick front is etched with black molding, and the somewhat elaborate yellow bottle-bottomed window is protected by sturdy burglar bars. Inside, there's more white brick with black molding, and an Internet jukebox that, because of the fantastic taste of BBL's patrons, plays the greatest selection of R&B and soul in the city—everything from Motown classics to Isley Brothers and Philly native Teddy Pendergrass (RIP). There's a back bricked-in patio out back that sometimes hosts a fish fry or crab boil when things outside are warm enough. For five dollars or thereabouts, you can snack on a fried whiting sandwich with hot and tartar sauces. It's truly a thing of beauty. Budweiser and cognac are the big sellers here, and the place goes through quite a bit of it, mostly because it never seems to close. The hours aren't posted, but the door never seems to be locked, even at 8 a.m. on a Tuesday morning.

Lots of retired, working class old timers drink their Bud at Billies, where they migrate from one of the dozen or so barber shops on 52nd around 5 or 6 o'clock, and carry on the same conversations they had earlier in the day, the soundtrack changing from the hum of clippers to the clink of bottles and the smooth voice of Smoky Robinson. After a few drinks, inevitably, someone will mention the time Obama spoke "Right. Out. Front." And then buy another round.

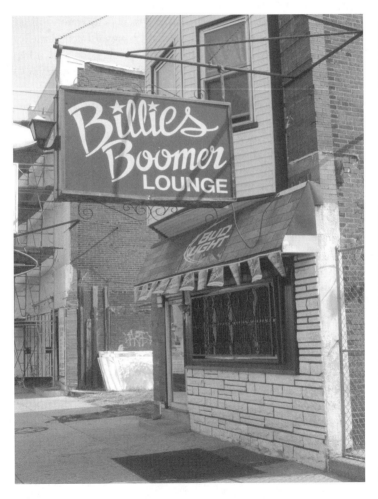

BJ Lounge

4027 Lancaster Ave.
Phone: 215-662-1090

In the half block walk from the train to BJ Lounge, I was hit up for money twice, both times by women, one of whom appeared to be pregnant. Looking around this block of Lancaster, you might assume a small bomb went off—there's trash everywhere, and it seems as if every other building is boarded up. When I tell the second woman that I just gave the last of my change to a woman up the street, she frowns, and asks instead for a promise that I'll pray for her. "Pray for Lisa Wyatt," she says, before rubbing her stomach. I don't ask if Lisa Wyatt is her name or the name of her child to be. I then head into a relatively empty BJ Lounge. But I have to be buzzed in first.

Beaten up red and black leather bar chairs with sturdy backs surround an oblong bar. There's a giant, glitter paint poster advertising the fast approaching first ever BJ beer and mussel fest. Just ten bucks will get you all the beer and mussels you can handle, a gray haired, slow-moving bartender tells me. "With music from Non-stop Rob!" However, there doesn't appear to be any place to make mussels inside BJ, which doesn't have a kitchen far as I can tell. Perhaps they'll make it a block party. But on this block, that doesn't sound like a great idea.

There's a real jukebox here, with Aretha's best alongside R. Kelly's *TP-2* and *Chocolate Factory*, as well as selections by other soul greats like the Isley Brothers and Marvin Gaye and jazz legends like Sonny Rollins. When the juke isn't being played, BJ Lounge is dead quiet. There's a man smoking a cigarette and drinking port wine over ice (a drink you'll see quite a bit of in West Philly) at the end of the bar, but he keeps to himself. Mirrors run the length of both sides of the bar, and hanging in front of the mirror on the right hand side of the entrance is a gigantic cigarette smoke filtration system called the Smokeeter which looks like it should be put on display at the Museum of Awesome. It's a relic from a bygone era; the slow moving bartender says has been there since the '70s.

The Phillies are on the TV, and Fox announcer Tim McCarver is working overtime to prove he's earned the URL created for him, shutuptimmccarver.com, by saying countless annoying things. Finally, the bartender snaps. "Motherfucker, we can count!" he says as he buzzes in a person at the door without bothering to check who it is.

Blue Nile Falls

720 S. 52nd St.
Phone: 215-747-9607

Dive Bar Rating

On the weekends, 52nd Street really lives up to its nickname as "West Philadelphia's Main Street." There are people everywhere, on foot, bike, skateboard, car, motorcycle, four-wheeler—any mode of transport you can think of. Give it enough time, and a roving gang of daredevils on dirt bikes and four-wheelers will come whizzing by, making all kinds of racket. You'll feel like you're in the middle of DMX's "Ruff Ryder's Anthem" video.

Blue Nile Falls sits smack dab in the middle of all the weekend chaos, just off the busy intersection of 52nd and Baltimore Avenue. Two stories tall, Blue Nile is both a bar and a restaurant. You can order beer and wine with your food upstairs, but mixed drinks are only available in the bar on the ground floor. Owner Demelash Demeshie is Ethiopian, and so too is the food Blue Nile serves. (Demelash's wife Delaynesh does all the cooking.) While there are several worthwhile Ethiopian eateries in the area—Dahlak, Queen of Sheeba, Abyssinia—that will satisfy your kit watt craving, Blue Nile is located the furthest west and as such, has less of a college student presence than the other spots.

Behind the bar are several vases with fake flowers in them. Christmas lights are hung up around the place for ambiance, and there's a giant can of Glade air freshener next to what seems like an endless supply of flavored rums and vodkas. (The smell of the bar is evidence that the bottle of Glade isn't going to last long.) Single bottles of Seagram are the big sellers, the music is loud and the conversation is louder. On the night I was here, a young woman tried to pay with a counterfeit $100 bill that had Abraham Lincoln's picture on it. Despite this slight error, she insisted she got the bill from the bank and thought that the note should still been honored by the bartender. Fat chance. "I don't care where it came from, honey," the bartender told her. "It. Is. Fake. I used to work at Wachovia, and we'd get burnt by fake money that looked real as shit. This ain't even *that*." Deterred, the young lady left in a huff, leaving her $100 Lincoln behind. It was passed around the bar in disbelief. "That's just lazy," someone said. "Lazy and stupid," another agreed.

Worst Bathrooms

DeLeo's Cafe

DiNic's Tavern

Pen & Pencil

Rosewood Tavern

Bonner's Irish Pub

McGlinchey's

Cookie's Tavern

Caprice Villa Lounge

5000 Market St.
Phone: 215-748-4499

Dive Bar Rating

When you pass Caprice Villa Lounge on the El train headed east from the 52nd Street station, the only sign you see is above the side entrance, which reads, rather simply and in block letters, HNIC. For those unawares, or without the sense to pick up Prodigy's stellar solo albums *HNIC Parts One* or *Two*, the acronym stands for Head Nigga In Charge, presenting an instant dilemma for customers of a lighter pigmentation. But pale patrons are rare at Caprice Villa, and in this neighborhood in general, a pocket of West Philly that's yet to be touched by the so called "Penntrification" that's sweeping west of the Schuylkill River and which has rebranded a huge swath of University City.

That's not to say the place is not welcoming, as bartender Carolyn or anyone pouring at Caprice will happily get you whatever you need. Caprice has been open for four decades, and celebrated its fortieth anniversary in April of 2010. The place has long been owned by the Hines family, and Willie Hines is the name on the paychecks nowadays. Framed pictures of the family hang around the bar, as does a plaque commemorating the life of family matriarch Lucy Hines, who lived to be 85 (January 19, 1922 – March 19, 2007). There are also lots of rules posted around the place. For instance, anyone caught using or selling drugs will be banned permanently. No hoodies. No loitering. No soliciting.

A few Dodge City video poker games dot the outside wall of the bar, and have "For Amusement Only" signs on them lest someone get drunk enough to forget they're in Pennsylvania and not Atlantic City. Upstairs, cooks fry fish and chicken, which you can smell walking up the street. Behind the bar is food of a less-delicious, but more affordable nature: giant pickles, Slim Jims and crackers. Behind them is a plaque that reads "HNIC June 18, 1980," and nearly all the hand written signs, "Door must remain closed," "Food upstairs," and the rules from the paragraph above, are signed HNIC as well.

I asked sweet Carolyn, pourer of the $3 Johnny Walker Black, what was up with all the HNIC stuff? "It means Head Nigga In

Charge." "Yes, I know, but why is it written on everything, and why is it on the sign above the door? What's its significance to Caprice Villa Lounge in particular?" The answer is in the bar's history: family owned for forty years, and nothing has been able to shut the joint down, not recession, not the drug trade outside its doors, not even the long and disastrous reconstruction of the El train, which cut business in half for over a year. HNIC it is then.

Cousin Danny's Exotic Haven

320 S. 52nd St.
No Phone

Dive Bar Rating

Just ten blocks away from Danny's, on May 13, 1985, then Mayor Wilson Goode Jr. dropped a bomb on a black political group known as MOVE. To this day, Philadelphia remains the only city in American history to ever drop a bomb on its own people. The wounds of that day still run deep. And as the push for Penntrification gobbles more and more real estate further and further west, the rhetoric gets more and more heated. "Keep West Philly Black!" is a phrase you might hear out this way. So too are bumper stickers that read, "This is West Philadelphia. University City is a marketing scheme."

Cousin Danny's Exotic Haven boasts that it's the oldest black owned strip club in Philadelphia. Don't know about that one, but it has been around for quite some time. (It was formerly called the Pony Tail.) Physically, it's a narrow place. A banquette to the left hugs the wall, while a shotgun bar to the right adorned with Christmas lights sticks out to accommodate for the stage and pole behind it. On that pole, for years, has been a dancer and West Philly institution named Big Kim. Kim is hefty—300 lbs plus if you had to put a number on it—but she can whirl around the pole with the best of them. She can also chug a full bottle of Corona with no hands, swallowing the last few ounces as she commands the bottle's neck to go in and out of her mouth and partly down her throat. It's a show that lives up to the tattoo on her arm: "52 Block Sexy."

The last time I was here, I brought my friend, Dave. We'd already been drinking for hours, and managed to talk our way out of the cover charge. As we walked in the narrow space between the barstools and banquet, one of the dancers said, "Evening, Officers," to us as we took our seats. A couple nights later Cousin Danny's bouncer, 27-year-old Orlando Morrison, was shot and killed while working the door. So, putting an officer inside might not be a bad idea.

Cousin Danny's Exotic Haven also has a Twitter account. Follow them @exotichaven for nuggets like this: "Your Tuesday nights will never be the same again cousindanny's presents $2 lap dance tuesdays also $2 wing platters." That's $4 for wings *and* breasts (though the only food I've seen in the place are never ordered Cup'o Noodles which sit behind the bar.)

El Toro Lounge

Dive Bar Rating

898 Belmont Ave
Phone: 215-477-1863

"Barack Obama is a part of the Black Illuminati," the girl next to me says. She's got a pierced tongue and eyebrow, and two girlfriends in tow. They nod approvingly. The words are heartfelt, and slurred. She's drunk. But she means what she says. "Oprah got Obama elected. She's part of the Black Illuminati too. They let him win so black folk would feel like we gettin' somewhere."

The bartender looks annoyed. "They've been talking about this all day," she says as she grabs my friend and me another beer. The woman doing most of the Black Illuminati talk—Jay Z and Kanye are also a part of it, as each use Illuminati symbols in their videos—then switches gears to a much more PC topic: Obama's homosexual agenda. All of this is being captured on two security cameras, and I want to ask the bartender if I can get a copy of the tape to view later, but don't dare.

El Toro is all wood walls, and a giant E Cast digital jukebox, which is shaped like an iPod—Paul Bunyan's iPod. Loads of glitter painted signs announce upcoming fish and chicken fries. There are hot dogs in a roaster behind the bar. Next to it, a sign that reads "Please do not Sit or Hang around in the Bar Unless You Have a Drink!!" During the lulls in Slurry Girl's Obama rants, Usher sings about his broken heart. He's got it, he's got it bad.

Eventually, we bid Slurry Obama Girl goodbye and walk into the wilds outside El Toro, into a West Philly neighborhood that's in severe disrepair. The row homes across the street look like they could be blown over if a strong enough gust of wind came by. Trash is picked up in wind gusts and blown to-and-fro. An old, closed and fenced in with barbed wire gas station sits next door to El Toro. In the window of the old place is a sign that advertises a couple of the things once-lucky shoppers could procure inside: "Wild Rabbits" and "Kerosene." Just thought that was worth mentioning.

Fiume

45th and Locust Sts.
No Phone

Dive Bar Rating

Fiume's location is truly a snapshot of how diverse pockets of West Philly have become. The place sits atop an Ethiopian restaurant called Abyssinia, a nod to the heavy African population in the area, as is the bar located across the street, Watusi II. You'll also find the newly-opened coffee shop Green Line Café across the street, and a block north you'll find, hands down, some of the best Falafel anywhere at Saad's Halal. A block lower and one block south is a tasty little gastro-pub with some serious beers of its own, Local 44.

With its new wood floor and mostly unadorned walls, Fiume is the size of a shoebox. A few tables are scattered about, and there are about five barstools, but chances are you'll be standing. There's no air conditioning, so box fans sitting inside open windows provide all the cooling in summer. As such, it feels a bit more New Orleans than West Philly. Citywide specials (Pabst and a shot of Beam) can be had for $3, and next to the bar you'll find tons of specialty brew packed tightly into a cooler which *you are not to touch*, even though it's as inviting as a flame to a moth. Those craft suds don't come cheap, but in a cramped, sometimes-sweaty, tiny room, they taste extra good.

Fiume also has a very deep selection of bourbon. The guy who runs the place, Kevin James Holland, is a connoisseur of the stuff, and is always eager to talk about new and exciting additions to his ever-expanding list, which he's been refining over the nine years the bar's been open. Every Thursday, he leads a group of musicians—known cleverly as The Citywide Specials—in country and bluegrass standards. On the Thursday I was here, the place was packed for them, and classics by Johnny Cash and (Pulitzer Prize winning) Hank Williams Sr. brought a tear to my beer.

Hide-A-Way Inn

51st St. and Hadfield
No Phone

Dive Bar Rating

It was country legend George Jones who once sang "a man can be a drunk sometimes, but a drunk can't be a man." And just inside the front door of Hide-A-Way, an exasperated woman is sending a man that very message. Loudly. He hasn't seen his kids in months. He's always at the bar. He's never home. He's trifling. The man just sits and takes it, not once opening his mouth, his silence the soundtrack to his guilt. After berating him for a good five minutes, the woman bluntly tells him to "fuck off ... forever," and heads out the door. The man surveys the room; everyone's trying hard not to look at him, but doing a lousy job of it. Then he drains the last of a fluorescent cocktail and sloughs off after her.

The rest of the patrons start laughing after he's gone, and one asks the bartender why she didn't intervene during the man's verbal beat down. "That's OPS," she says. "Other People's Shit." As the lone white guy in the bar, she feels the need (why, I don't know) to offer her apologies to me, saying that that type of thing usually doesn't happen at Hide-A-Way. I know this already, as I've been here once before. That time I was drunker than the guy being told off, so I'd come back during this relatively quiet (except for the unhappy couple) happy hour.

Hide-A-Way is famous for a wheel they keep behind the bar. Patrons pay a dollar to spin it, and win whatever prize is in the slot the wheel stops on. The catch is, nothing on the wheel is worth a dollar; prizes, I was told by a guy who'd been here several times, could be a loaf of white bread or a couple of cans of tuna fish. On neither one of my visits have I seen the wheel spun.

The jukebox gets a workout here, and the shot gun bar and the leather banquette that runs alongside it eventually fill up with people happy to show off their dance moves. Of the cocktails I've seen imbibed, none seem to be of a color that appears in nature—shocking neon greens, electric blues, fluorescent reds. Have enough of those things, and winning a loaf of white bread might seem like a good deal.

Melody Lounge

51st St. and Haverford Ave.
Phone: 215-747-5138

Dive Bar Rating

God bless the rail thin, pencil mustached Vietnam vet who lives next door to Melody Lounge. He comes in to the bar each and every day. Everyone here likes him quite a bit, and they all respect what he's done for our country. Yet, no one wants to talk to him.

Let's put that another way: no one can talk to him. Because no one can understand what he's saying—ironically, the only two phrases that are clear are "Catch my drift?" and "Know what I mean?" He's got a diamond stud in his left ear, and wears a crucifix around his neck, which he kisses sometimes. When he does, you'll think he must've just talked about Jesus, though you can't really be sure. He wears a royal blue trucker promoting Prescor Inc, a company based in Tulsa, Oklahoma that presses hot steel discs into tank heads using hydraulic presses. After he leaves, the patrons of Melody argue over whether or not he ever worked there or if he just copped the hat in a thrift store somewhere. "I asked him once," one of them says. "Couldn't understand his answer."

Fake flower arrangements dot the rectangular bar. *Cops* is playing on the large screen TV and some of those watching debate what drugs the perps being arrested are on while talking about their own run-ins with the law. It's an older crowd, mainly very friendly retirement-aged folks who sip their port over ice quietly and talk about their particular nook of West Philly. Fridays and Saturdays they have a big crab boil at Melody, and that brings people out. They pack tightly elbow to elbow inside its four ridged wood walls, stepping out occasionally to smoke.

Before trying to leave, I let a couple guys I'm talking to know I'm heading over to the bar caddy-corner from Melody, Cozy's Lounge. "Oh, no," they both say. "Don't go over there." They then explain to me that Cozy's is a young man's bar, and young men can't control their liquor. They drink too much, begin to think they're Superman, and one mistaken look or misinterpreted word can end in violence. "They act a fool over there at Cozy's. I wouldn't go if I was you, at least not at night." So I don't. With people this nice here, and all the crab you can eat, why the hell would I?

New 3rd World Lounge

4900 Baltimore Ave.
Phone: 215-476-1515

The New 3rd World Lounge gives no indication that it's open for business. The phone number doesn't work. What windows it has are boarded up. You never see anyone going in an out of it, particularly during the day, when I've stopped by nearly a dozen times to find the door locked.

The Brooklyn spazzy noise trio Genghis Tron lived in Philadelphia for just over a year. When they did, they lived just across the street from New 3rd World. They used to swear it would open sporadically on weekends. Another friend who lives close by has vouched for this. He lived behind the place, and told tales of drug deals at odd hours at night and random gunfire every few weeks. It was a notorious drug den, he told me, and according to him, its "are they closed for good?" status is a perfectly played possum move on their part. If you need something at New 3rd World Lounge, you know when to go. If you don't, they don't want you around anyway.

So imagine my surprise when, on a trip one night to the liquor store close by, I saw a guy out front of New 3rd World, the door open, and lights on inside. I briefly wondered, given what I'd been told about the place, if they would even let me in. Maybe there's a secret handshake, or knowing nod that proves to them I'm *down*?

But, nah, none of that. For all the hoopla and whispers about the place, it's fairly normal. It's cozy even. The building's exterior—falling down sign, peeling paint, boarded windows—is the reason the rumors gained traction in the first place. It doesn't make a good first impression. But inside, its loud, conversations are spirited and there's a dance party breaking out to old soul tracks and a bit of world music thrown in for good measure. The doorman and the bartender have thick African accents, which makes sense in this part of the city, and the clientele seems to be made largely of African immigrants as well.

I struck up a conversation with a young man whose name I won't attempt to spell. He was from Nigeria originally, and drove a cab. He told me a story about a young couple he'd picked up a couple nights prior. He was taking them to her house, and the two of them were kissing feverishly, to the point where he thought he might have to tell them "No sex in my cab." But, suddenly and without warning, the girl puked all over the guy. "I charge them $10 extra," he said smiling, before a young woman pulled him onto the dance floor.

New Angle Lounge

3901 Lancaster Ave.
Phone: 215-387-5147

Dive Bar Rating

When it comes to the bar she runs, Florence Furman is blunt. "No kids!" When she says "kids," she's not talking about age, as you have to be 21 to get in the New Angle, just like at any other bar. As a matter of fact, a good percentage of the bar's patronage comes from nearby Drexel University, so college-aged "kids" can be found in the joint on most nights. No, what Furman is talking about is maturity, meaning if you're coming here to fuck around, don't come. "This is a no nonsense bar," she says. "Come out to drink and have a good time, and we'll be alright with you."

Florence's mother LaTanya has owned New Angle (which is also sometimes referred to as "The Triangle") for thirty-nine years, and the clientele has changed several times over that time, from black to white and back again and then back again. In the '90s, the place was a punk rock hang. These days, it's a healthy racial mix of older working class blacks and Drexel students and professors. "Mature people," as Florence calls them. As the day wears on, the crowd gets younger. That's due in part to the themed nights that have less appeal to old timers looking to sip their suds in relative peace. "Rocky Wednesdays" features dollar cans of Coors Light and a vague *Rocky* theme, and every once in awhile they'll have a mojito night. "Best mojito in town," says Florence.

There's no food at New Angle, so the bar qualifies for Philly's smoking exemption, which states that smoking is allowed in bars that can show they derive less than 20 percent of their revenue from food. The exemption was made when the smoking ban passed in 2007, but Florence just put in her paperwork to get the license in the summer of 2010, she says. She'll know soon whether or not she's been approved. Until then, just come in, and act in a mature fashion.

Parkside Inn

52nd and Parkside Ave.
No Phone

Fresh Prince wasn't the only famous rapper to come out of West Philly. There was also Schoolly D, and one of his most well-known songs, "Parkside 5-2," off his venerable 1987 LP *Saturday Night! The Album* (named one of the best hip-hop albums of all time by *The Source*) will be bumping in your head when you saddle up to the bar at the Parkside Inn, on the corner of 52nd St and Parkside Avenue. This was Schoolly's hood and in "Parkside 5-2" the Parkside Inn gets a shout out. "Drove to the corner to see my homeboy Lynn/ crusin' round the corner to the Parkside Inn/ Jumped out the car/ Ran into the bar/ About six or seven steps 'cuz it wasn't too far."

Schoolly left this neighborhood long ago. He now lives on Philadelphia's affluent Main Line, drinks turmeric tea every morning, practices yoga and eats for three reasons—health, sex and vanity—according to a food diary he kept recently for Grub Street Philadelphia. He's a certified yuppie. But his beloved Parkside remains relatively unchanged.

The bar is a cavernous two stories high. The walls are black, and once inside you'll forget sunlight exists. It's *dark*. A giant iPod shaped jukebox is attached to the wall by the door, and it's so loud that sometimes the bass booming out of the PA rattles the rickety building. Across the street is one of Philadelphia's most beautiful concert venues, the Mann Center for Performing Arts. The Philly Chamber Orchestra performs there, and just a stone's throw from where Schoolly D's friend Mike used to sell weed, Aretha Franklin performed, with Condeleeza Rice accompanying her on piano. Doubt either of them made their way across the street to Parkside for a cocktail. If they had, they would've gotten friendly service from any number of women spilling out of too-tight dresses.

Queen of Sheba II

4511 Baltimore Ave
Phone: 215-382-2099

Dive Bar Rating

Can we spend a few sentences talking about the lost art of the juke-box? They hardly exist anymore, at least in the traditional sense, as now, more than ever, bars (and especially dives) jut strap that odious Touch Tunes Internet juke on the wall and call it a day. It's an easy call, I suppose. There's a wider selection, and that should be a good thing. But it's not.

In some places, it works. At Billies Boomer, HNIC, Burgs and the like, Touch Tunes offers a bigger slice of awesome for the old heads to pick through, and often to perfect results. Isley Brothers followed by Kelis is not a bad thing. But most times, this wide a spectrum is more tragic and frightening than a baby running on ice with a pair of scissors—like the chunk of Gavin Rosedale at Fireside Tavern, or at OMACs, where its owner followed R. Kelly's "Real Talk" with a song from Jared Leto's abysmal 30 Seconds to Mars. It's just too much power to give to a person who lacks taste, and has been drinking ten or more $1.50 Lagers a day for the better part of his or her life. In the end, a jukebox with preselected music is what works best, adding to a dive's character.

Queen of Sheba II has a real jukebox, and its chock full of fantastic stuff: Isley Brother's *Eternal* (also in Oscar's incredible jukebox), Erykah Badu, Jerry Butler, Marvin Gaye. The bar itself is a lovely place on West Philly's lovely Baltimore Avenue, which, over the last few years, has undergone a very lovely rejuvenation. In less than a mile down Baltimore, you'll pass lovely Clark Park, which is adjacent to the lovely Green Line Café coffee shop, where people sip their caffeine outdoors and new, young and lovely parents push baby strollers. All around the park, incredibly large Victorian loom like the wallpaper in an architects' wet dream, and an Amish farmers market sets up shop on the weekend. Down a bit is another market, Milk and Honey, the place to go for overpriced organic produce and locally sourced cheese and meat. Up a few blocks comes the spice of Baltimore Avenue, its African grocery stores and Ethiopian and Indian restaurants. Gojjo serves up great vegetarian Ethopian fare, and has, of late, become a hot spot for live jazz. Just blocks away there's a yoga studio and Gold Standard, a nice brunch place. And, in the middle of this loveliness is Queen of Sheba II, which also features its own pretty serviceable Ethiopian food. And, it bears repeating, a real goddamn jukebox.

Besides the jukebox, what's really great here is the chance to down a citywide special (shot of Beam with a PBR) for $3 at any hour of the day or night. They sell Milwaukee's Best pounders here for $3 too, and little colored light bulbs backlighting the bar almost give it a cantina feel. In the dining room across a half wall with an homage to Pabst Blue Ribbon in stain glass are posters of the Great Kings of Africa, and pictures of Barack Obama. In back, is the kitchen with an open window facing the bar and dining room; the spicy, soothing smells ooze out of it, filling up the room. Fantastic place. Lovely, even.

Smitty's Millcreek Tavern

52nd and Wyalusing
No Phone

Everyone around the bar at Smitty's Millcreek Tavern is drinking the same exact thing: Taylor's port wine, over ice, with a slice of lemon. As a matter of fact, they keep giant jugs of it behind the bar. While they have other stuff too—Thunderbird, Wild Irish Rose, even a big bottle of Mad Dog 20/20 orange jubilee—its Taylor's over ice, garnished with lemon, that's getting all the love. Of course, that could be because they serve it in the most gigantic glass you've ever seen, glasses that could give beer steins in Munich a complex.

The walls at Smitty's—tagline "It's a family affair"—are lime green, and flecked with bits of green tile. There's a giant digital juke attached to the back wall that's so loud the big bottles of Taylor shake a bit when a song plays. If there's a game on—Phillies, Eagles—they'll turn the thing off, which is great because you'll then get running game commentary from the old timers around the bar. Such as: the drinkers around the bar all grumble when Ryan Howard strikes out in a game against the Braves. You see, he's just signed a $25 million dollar a year contract, and everyone at the bar is trying to figure out how much he just made in the time it took for him to strike out. Howard turned thirty in November of 2009, someone says. This prompts the guy sitting next to him to say, "I'm 33 and I don't have $3."

Behind the bar is a picture of Smitty, Millcreek's owner, as well as a sign—next to a jar of giant dill pickles—announcing that the place is a "member's only" establishment. There's a "members only" group trip planned for Atlantic City later in the month, the bartender explains without offering any details about what it takes to become a member. There's also a back room filled with video poker that it says you have to be twenty-five or older to enter, though a shirtless, heavily-tattooed young kid walks right in without any hassle. Later on, a guy comes in selling bootleg DVDs. No one's buying, so he sits down and orders a drink. I'll give you three guesses what he had.

Watusi Pub II

232 S. 45th St.
Phone: 215-243-9389

Just across the street from Fiume and trendy coffee shop Green Line Café, Watusi Pub II—known simply as "Watusi II" to its regulars—has been open for nearly a quarter century. The spacious joint has two levels, and a large rectangular bar spans the length of the first level and has fifty or so stools that fill up on the weekends with an aged, African American clientele. Rows of dollar bills sit just beneath the bar's lacquered finish, which is surrounded by a handsome brass rail. Up a flight of ten or so stairs is another bar, which plays host to spirited karaoke on Tuesdays courtesy of TNT Productions. Two old window units do an admirable job of keeping the whole place cool in the summer months. One of them sits just above the main entrance and leaks quite a bit, so you'll be lucky to come in or leave without getting a tad wet. On hotter days, a giant industrial fan in the corner helps pick up the slack for the leaking AC (things can get a bit gusty on the side of the bar the fan is on).

A steady stream of old hits plays on the digital jukebox. You'll hear a fairly steady mix of Gap Band and P Funk with the occasional modern hit by Jay Z or Usher thrown in. The walls are relatively unadorned save for two African masks above the staircase in back, and some elegant, old-world lighting fixtures that give clues that the building used to be a hotel. There are also frequent specials. Monday night sees all beer going for $2, while Thursdays are two for one cocktails, bottom or top shelf.

Occasionally, spillover from the usually-crowded Fiume across the street will seep in for a drink or two, and a bartender with tattoos on both of her huge breasts (one of a four leaf clover, the other of a … oops, caught me lookin') says that students from nearby Penn and Drexel come in every once in a blue moon to scope out the place. There is also a Watusi I, up a block on 46th and Walnut. It's much nicer than its twin, with a brand new awning and a top-flight menu. Signs on the wall at Watusi II let you know parties held within its walls can be catered by its prettier sister up the street.

Way's Lounge

3851 Lancaster Ave.
Phone: 215-222-7107

Dive Bar Rating

On a Saturday afternoon during the never-ending heat wave that was the Philadelphia summer of 2010, Way's Lounge is empty. Owner Wayman Seal III—"Butch" to his friends—is just about to close up shop for the day, but is happy not to. The air inside is cold and crisp. Butch has owned Way's Lounge—a gorgeous old-school wood-paneled joint on Lancaster—since 1986, when he bought it from Charles "Homie" Johnson. Back then it was called Homie's Spot. Before it was Homie's, it was Lloyd's Lounge. Before that, in the 1950s, it was called the Pink Slipper. But it's Butch's now, and large blown up pictures of him and his wife of over forty-five years, Lucille, adorn the walls behind the bar. Next to them are a couple of hand-written signs: "Absolutely no drugs allowed" and "Please pay when served. No tabs here." Around the bar are tiny brass light fixtures with red light bulbs poking out of them. In the middle of the week, from 8 to 11pm, customers can have a shot of anything on the bottom or middle shelf for a buck, for what Butch appropriately calls "$1 Wednesdays." All happy hours are two drinks for the price of one.

The bar at Way's is shotgun, and when it's slow, Butch might spend more time on your side of it than on his own. He can see the TV better that way. There are a few old world touches here that are easily appreciated, like the elegant red leather door that leads to the men's restroom (Butch says it was there when he bought the place). Way's used to host live jazz combos, but doesn't anymore. They're a block down from New Angle, which caters to the students at Drexel with theme nights and specials on Coors Light. Way's doesn't do all that, so sun up or down the clientele remains the same. Speaking of old world touches…

Peck Miller's Bar *(Bill Koneski)*

MANAYUNK/ROXBOROUGH/ OFF THE BEATEN PATH

Cheers

69th and Market Street
No Phone

Dive Bar Rating

🍾🍾🍾🍾🍾

The most interesting thing about Cheers in Upper Darby isn't the bar itself, but its owner, 70-year-old Robert Herdelin. He's been called a slum lord by Upper Darby Police Superintendent Michael Chitwood, and his bar a "nuisance," "the worst in the area," a "pit" and a "shoot 'em up joint for drugs and weapons." The place was raided by the police on March 26, 2010, who arrested two known drug dealers and a few under aged drinkers. A week before the raid, a shootout between two *other* drug dealers took place in the restroom, leaving one person dead.

About all this, Herdelin is nonplussed. What's he supposed to do, he asks, check everyone's pockets for drugs and guns when they walk through the door? He estimates that he throws out a drug dealer a week on average already, and it's not his fault that the neighborhood has fallen to shit. He lives above the bar in a tiny, cramped one-bedroom apartment, and has for most of the twenty-seven years he's owned the place. He's seen the neighborhood crumble first hand.

Now here's the kicker: Herdelin is a millionaire. He owns several big-deal rental properties on the Jersey shore, one of which he rented to Oprah for a cool $16,000 a week. That he chooses to live where he does, picking fistfights with drug dealers in a neighborhood he's already written off and says he'll leave soon, speaks to his peculiar nature and also the fact that he's a very unabashed spendthrift. It's why Cheers looks like it might fall down at any moment and why the door to the bathroom stall doesn't get fixed. Herdelin would rather hold on to the cash.

About that bar: it's located just up the street from the Tower Theater, a venerable venue that's had acts as diverse as Willie Nelson, Erykah Badu, David Bowie and Radiohead on its stage. The crowd at Cheers on any given night will generally reflect whose name is on the marquee a half a block away, as not only is it the only bar within walking distance of the Tower (there are bars inside the place, but we're talking $9 bottles of Miller Lite), but it's certainly the only one that has pictures behind the bar of its 70-year-old owner wearing a Speedo and flexing his pecks. Yes, Herdelin is one crazy loon—a crazy loon who just slapped Superintendent Chitwood with a $1.7 million libel lawsuit. If he wins, you better believe he'll keep the money in a shoebox under his mattress.

Most Intimidating

Commodore Lounge

Billy's Chili Pot

DeLeo's Café

Jack's Famous Bar

Dolphin Tavern

DiNic's Tavern

Burg's Lounge

Cousin Danny's Exotic Haven

1201 Bar

Old Philadelphia Bar

Cresson Inn

114 Gay Street
No Phone

Dive Bar Rating

🍾🍾🍾

Manayunk was one of the original twelve Philadelphia Townships that were formed from land granted by William Penn in 1680. The area was known as Flat Rock back then—and for a blink Udorovia— but its name was permanently changed to Manayunk in 1824, from the Indian words meaning "where we go to drink." No bullshit. The area was incorporated by the City of Philadelphia in 1854 as the 21st ward, and while The Cresson Inn—or, "the Cresson," as locals call it—may not have been there back then, it sure feels like it was. It's still even got its "Ladies Entrance" sign up, from when the bar was separated from a dining room. Women weren't allowed where liquor was served.

The place is preserved in amber, unchanged as everything around it morphs into a yuppie utopia. A block away from the bar— which is located on the corner of Gay and Cresson streets and tucked under an elevated regional rail line—on Main Street, college kids dart in and out of boutique clothiers, cyclists don $150 Oakley shades while riding their $3,000 Cannondale carbon bicycles, young parents push strollers and well dressed professionals dine al fresco. Of course, Manayunk also owns the dubious distinction of being the place where frat boys love to play, so the area can be overrun by gaggles of popped collared, flip flop and backward baseball cap wearing college-aged assholes who can't hold their liquor and end up starting fistfights and pissing in the streets. But you wouldn't guess that from inside the Cresson, whose tagline is "Where The Real Yunkers Drink" (Real is underlined). The bar has retained all of its blue collar dive-y charm, and remains a solid option for anyone seeking to sip a cold one without getting price gouged or exposed to the radiation that seeps out of most of the douche-tastic bars in this burg.

Dotting the walls are old framed black and white photos of the neighborhood from decades past. There's a Touch Tunes digital jukebox which seems to be permanently (and regrettably) locked on Eminem, but thankfully this doesn't irritate the bar staff, who are cordial as they come. (They'll even apologize if you have to ask them for a clean glass.) Unfortunately, some nods to the area frat culture have crept inside here. There's a SoCo and Lime shot machine behind the bar, and they've started serving $2 Michelob Ultras during sporting events. Both are cancelled out, somewhat, by a sign behind the bar warning pregnant patrons that they won't be served, as though at some point that was such an issue here that someone decided a sign was needed to stomp it out. Now that's <u>Real</u>.

DeLeo's Café

405 Dupont St.
Phone: 215-482-9784

Dive Bar Rating

🍾🍾🍾🍾🍾

Poor guy. He'd barely stuck his head in the door before he was being admonished with a loud, angry chorus of *"Nooooo!"* from the bartender, the six or so daytime drinkers scattered around the rectangular bar and the four guys playing pool. "You're flagged, motherfucker!" yelled one man, pointing a pool cue violently. "Motherfucker, you're flagged," the bartender screamed, shooing the guy away with an unopened can of Miller Lite. Finally, the whole bar shouted in unison: *"FLAGGED!"* The poor guy blinked slowly, absorbing the blow, and then withdrew back into the sunlight outside.

Welcome to DeLeo's *Café*, the divey-est of all the working-class dives on the Manayunk/Roxbourgh cusp. They don't take kindly to strangers here, as non-regulars are gazed upon openly and with suspicion. Some of the regulars actually physically recoil in the presence of newcomers, hovering nervously around their drinks and waiting uncomfortably for the intruder to leave so they can go back to being themselves. Others take the opposite tack, turning the asshole meter to eleven, puffing their chests and cursing loudly with gusto.

While it may be called DeLeo's Cafe, it's not a restaurant. Hell, it's barely even a bar. Talk Roxborough/Manayunk dives—Peck Miller's Bar, Pop Pop's II, Cresson Inn—to anyone who knows and DeLeo's will come heavily "recommended," with equal measures of sarcasm and caution. "It's a *reaalll* classy joint. Make sure you put your wallet in your front pocket." "Top notch. Don't make eye contact." There's a distinct B.O. funk in the air that suits the place perfectly as in the last few years, it's been written up by the city for fruit-fly, roach, mouse and spider infestation. Also, for not cleaning their utensils properly, which seems redundant, as they've also been cited for not having a proper sink for sanitation.

But at this moment, no one is thinking about any of that, as they're all shaking their heads, marveling at the gall of the Poor Guy, coming back here, and so soon. So what'd he do to get flagged? "He smeared his own shit all over the walls and floor of the women's restroom," the bartender answers, his mouth switching back and forth between gleeful smirk and bitter disgust. So. that is what you have to do to get banned here.

Five Points Cocktail Lounge

4091 Ford Rd.
Phone: 215-879-6899

Dive Bar Rating

Five Points Cocktail Lounge is located at the cross section of Monument Road, Ford Road and Conshohocken Avenue. While Monument and Ford keep stretching beyond Five Points, Conshohocken dead ends in front of it, and so when you're out front of this saucy, boisterous lounge, five different stretches of road intersect right in front of you.

Beside the entrance is a gold plaque that reads "In memory of Wayne Lewis." Inside, signs urge customers to sign up for Five Points' "Dirty 9" softball team and to come out to one of the many events going on at the bar, including "Big Poppa Georgie Oldies But Goodies Fish Fry," where Poppa himself will be spinning the best soul and R&B from back in the day, and Karaoke Wednesdays featuring MC Blue.

Once inside people, mostly older, dance to loud hits—be they contemporary fare by R. Kelly or old school joints like the Temptations "The Way You Do the Things You Do"—or play pool in back. A monstrous rectangular bar fills the room, and behind it, two sexy bartenders in tight-fitting outfits pour giant Big Gulp size cocktails that are as pretty as the ocean is deep, each a different shade of red, green or blue. I ask for what the lady next to me is having, and am poured a red, sweet concoction. I don't ask what it is, and the bartender doesn't tell me. It's sweet and tangy in equal parts, and cheap—six bucks—for its sheer volume and heft. The drink isn't near as sweet, however, as the half dozen or so old couples dancing arm and arm to whatever tumbles out of the Touch Tunes Jukebox. They twirl and dip. This place is swingin'. Wherever Wayne Lewis is, he's surely proud.

Peck Miller's Bar

6119 Ridge Ave.
Phone: 215-483-5719

Dive Bar Rating

The bartender slides a drink in front of me and scans the room suspiciously. "I just poured you a double by accident, baby. I'll only charge you for a single, but don't mention it because my boss is here and he wouldn't like that." I thank her, and toss her a large tip, before she gives me one of her own. Namely, "don't eat the hot dogs." There are a dozen or so rotating on a little 7- Eleven style spit behind the left hand side of a bar that's shaped like a backward and very erect capital C if you're looking at it from the front entrance. "They were put on at 8 a.m. this morning, I'd guess." It's now nine at night, so the advice is appreciated. "Matter of fact," she says, staring at the blistered dogs, "I'm going to put on some new ones and throw those away." She pulls up a trash can and starts spearing each with a fork, dismayed that the morning shift bartender cut little notches up them to make them cook more quickly. "I think it looks gross," she says, furrowing her brow. "They look like worms."

Across the bar, one drunk man is telling another about the time he was attacked with a lead pipe. They hit him twice in the head, broke his arm, and hit him in the leg. Elsewhere in the confines of Peck Miller's mostly unadorned walls, a man in an Eagles' jersey three sizes too big is getting very serious about a game of shuffle board bowling he's started with two women who look freshly plucked from an '80s-era Whitesnake video. He's high on something (maybe the Aqua Net fumes emanating off his rivals), and his eyes are wild. "Youse are my guys," he says to the girls before he begins telling them tales of badass shuffle board bowling games past. "Remember, we needed two strikes in a row to win, and *we did it*." These memories see him erupt with glee; he kisses the suit of armor by the bar's front door, and orders another shot of blackberry brandy. He's "accidentally" poured a double too, but doesn't seem to notice. He asks for a hot dog. "Sure," the bartender says before sticking one of the last remaining worms on the rotating spindles. "Here ya go."

Pop Pop's II

7168 Ridge Ave.
Phone: 215-483-9129

Pop Pop's II is the home of the $2.50 forty of Piels, so you can get mighty plowed here mightily cheaply, and most people here, even midday on a Sunday, are just that.

The place has got a great jukebox—ZZ Top, Sinatra, the best of Yes (!). At one point, George Thorogood's "Bad to the Bone" starts blaring, and a man at the bar starts singing the chorus to the woman he's with, changing the words slightly. "I'm bad with my bone," he says to her, pressing his nose to hers. There's also a woman dancing wildly to whatever comes on, about to bounce right out of her Rolling Stones' shirt. She all but loses her mind when Foreigner's "Double Vision" is punched up. If you ever feel half as passionate about anything in life as she does about the opening line—"Feelin' down and dirty, feelin' kinda mean"—you'll do just fine. There's talk around the bar that a regular has locked himself in the bathroom again. The bartender knocks on the door and tells him he'll be "flagged" if he doesn't get his stinkin' ass outta there right fuckin' now. The guy obliges, sitting down at the bar and lighting up a cigarette as if nothing's happened.

There's also a guy named Billy, who sits at the end of the bar, sipping his beer quietly. He looks as though he's been caught in a dust storm, and occasionally he'll get up, pick up a case of beer, walk behind the bar, and stock a cooler. He's got one of the most impressive beer guts you'll ever see, all hard and perfectly round. "Billy stole my basketball and won't give it back," a man who catches me staring says as he rubs Billy's impressive mound. Beach ball made of steel would be more like it.

Billy's Chili Pot

GREAT NORTHEAST

Beef Seekers Inn

3234 Red Lion Rd
Phone: 215-637-1444

Dive Bar Rating

The Great Northeast section of Philadelphia has long possessed a separate identity from the rest of the city. Populated by Irish Catholics and Russian immigrants, it's the only part of Philadelphia where the Republican Party has gained any traction over the years. Republican State Senator Hank Salvatore even introduced a bill in 1980s that would have allowed the Northeast to secede from the rest of Philly and rechristen itself Liberty County. Northeast residents favored the bill four to one. Fortunately, or unfortunately, depending on your viewpoint, it never went to vote.

Much of the discontent stems from geography, as residents here feel disconnected from the goings on at City Hall and in Center City. "We pay taxes, residents would gripe, and for what?" the *Inquirer* wrote of the general feelings of Northeast residents in 2004. "The money goes to Center City/North Philadelphia/Anywhere But Here. Our trash collection is substandard, the police are too busy in other parts of Philadelphia to respond to our complaints, and don't even ask us about getting snow removed." Some believe there's a racial element to all this, too, and that the real reason many choose to live in the area is because they find the more-ethnically-mixed parts of the city unbearable. To wit, there's a bar here called Casper's Place, which I've been told by a native of the neighborhood, used to sell shirts that read "No Spooks Allowed."

The two old friends fighting at the end of the bar at Beef Seekers aren't doing much to dispel rumors of the Northeast's racism, latent or otherwise, as they pepper their argument with copious use of the N-word for seemingly no reason. No one around the bar bats an eye at their fight, which is getting pretty serious. "I'm depending on you! It's for my son's birthday! Do this for me and I will forgive your debt and forget you lied to me! That's the big thing here! You don't lie to friends!" The guy getting the earful, much younger than the man dishing it out, just nods. "I'll do it. I'll do it. You're right. You're right," he finally says.

The bar is located in a strip mall behind a Wendy's and a Dunkin

Donuts, tucked next to an H&R Block, a Rite Aid and an Acme. It's actually a glorious dive, if you can stomach the language. The place has great wood walls, and nearly all the old timers inside are doing their part to cake them with secondhand cigarette smoke. The drink of choice here is a pint of Bud with a shot of Canadian Club poured in. Giant softball trophies stand proud and tall behind the bar, and bartender Bob is a soft-spoken gent with a buzz cut and a penchant for being direct. I ask him about the origin of the bar's name. His answer is quite literal. A guy came in here once. He was tired of eating spaghetti. He wanted a steak. They made him one.

Billy's Chili Pot Inc.

4738 Frankford Ave.
Phone: 215-744-2905

Dive Bar Rating

🍾🍾🍾🍾🍾

Whenever I call Billy's Chili Pot Inc. on the phone, a drunk customer seems to answer. This makes it difficult to get my questions about the place answered. For instance, does Billy's Chili Pot actually serve chili? I've heard it doesn't. Oh, it does? Twelve kinds, you say? The most popular being Jim Bob's, which features spice and everything nice, but mostly Jim Bob? [click]

To get to Billy's Chili Pot requires a considerable trek up the Market-Frankford El to the Margaret-Orthodox stop, just short of where the line ends. A trip this far up the El isn't advisable, and generally only people looking to cop serious drugs or seeking to be murdered by someone looking to cop serious drugs aren't off the line by Allegheny. While that may sound like wild hyperbole, all the proof you'll need to see that it isn't is to get off at Margaret-Orthodox and start walking about looking for Billy's. A quick call to figure out which direction up Frankford to walk will be met with a "Who the hell wants to know?" The answer is about half a block northeast, and you'll want to pick up the pace as you pass women tweaking on meth or high on crack dancing in front of cars trying their best to get around them. Still more folks with what appears to be itchy skin dart in an out of abandoned storefronts, or appear from out of nowhere right in front of you from behind the large cement columns holding up the train line.

Once you reach Billy's, a group of Puerto Ricans will tell you that the cover is $15, only they're not with Billy's, but instead are running (what appears to be) an illegal club out of their apartment next door, the booming music blaring out of it the only thing louder than the train rumbling by above. By the time you do get inside Billy's you'll feel a sense of relief, as the place is an oasis from the madness outside, an oasis that does indeed sell chili. But not tonight. Tonight they've got boiled eggs for 35 cents apiece that are served in a Styrofoam bowl with a shaker of salt. Bartender Mary is sweet enough. Pints of Lager are $2.

The place is bright and old men surround the bar. There are booths in back and the two TVs are tuned to sports. There's a shuffleboard bowling game in the very backend of the bar that doesn't work, and a Harley Davidson Pinball machine that does. On the left wall in back are what seem to be thirty years of softball plaques commemorating various Billy's Chili Pot teams over the years, everything from first place to thanks for showing up.

Then, suddenly, there's a very loud THWACK. One of the old men has fallen face first onto the floor and is knocked out cold. A couple of other men stumble to his aid and wonder aloud if they should call him a taxi or an ambulance. One of the men notices the Harley Pinball for what seems to be the first time, leaves his fallen comrade and drops some change in the machine, playing with the unconscious old man at his feet. After a few spooky minutes, the old man finally comes to, but doesn't seem to understand a word being said to him. He then stumbles out into the wilds of the night, nearly falling again before he gets to the exit. "There's no way he's going to make it home," a man from the bar says. Thinking about it, I start to feel sick. Though it may just be the smell of the hardboiled egg my friend Brian has just eaten.

City Line Bar & Horseshoe Pits

9961 Frankford Ave
Phone: 215-637-7800

Dive Bar Rating

Above the bar at City Line Bar & Horseshoe Pits is a sign that reads "Just say no to crack...and rap." It reminds me of a time, long ago, at a bar called Carol's in Philly's burbs, when a patron was warned by the bartender not to play another song by DMX. He did, and the bartender unplugged the jukebox. "You don't listen too fuckin' good, do ya?" The difference between that bartender and the one pouring at City Line Bar & Horseshoe Pits—so named because it's right next to the City Line bus stop...and there are horseshoe pits in the parking lot out back—is that the bartender here can barely pour a drink, much less do the deep knee bend it would require to unplug the jukebox across the room. She seems to be suffering from a serious case of the DTs.

Everyone at City Line smokes. None of them have ashtrays. Instead they drop their ash into tiny plastic cups half filled with water. Thus, cups of floating, bloated wet butts are everywhere, all over the bar, on every table. My friend Doug surveys the room and asks, "Is it just me, or does every woman in this place look pregnant?" He's got a point. Bartender with the shakes, pregnant looking women, two kids who don't look a day over fifteen playing pool: This place is sketch city.

That said, there's a bit of sweet mixed into the sour. An older couple dance closely to Michael McDonald's "What A Fool Believes," exchanging long glances and a couple of kisses. This prompts two young guys playing pool to mime as though they're about to puke. Out front, a young white couple are sitting in the back of an open trunk, drinking bottles of Miller Lite. Both are wearing the same outfit—white tank tops, basketball shorts, white tube socks and Adidas shower shoes. She's quietly sobbing. Maybe someone close to her has died? Maybe this young man is breaking her heart in the back of this trunk, telling her it's over, that he will be trunk drinking with someone else from now on? Or maybe she mistook one of those cups of wet cigarette butts for her cocktail?

Leneghan's Crusader Inn

Dive Bar Rating

7412 Frankford Avenue
Phone: 215-338-7700

Leneghan's Crusader Inn is the place that Al Bundy types looking to relive their high school glories go to commiserate. The bar is mostly Irish in theme—green walls and shamrocks painted throughout—though there is quite a bit of memorabilia from the Father Judge Crusaders, the local high school team around these parts, here too. The team's football helmet, emblazoned with a cross, can be found in several of the framed photos hanging on the walls. At a tiny entry way up front, stacks of Father Judge football season schedules sit next to copies of Penny Saver newspapers.

Before I enter, a tweaker dressed oddly in all Celtics gear tries to convince me there's a cover charge of $5, but he's just kidding. On weeknights, there's not much atmosphere; no music, only the sound of Jay Leno's flop sweat as he butchers his way through an unfunny monologue. A few of the drunks around the bar are laughing though, in particular a man with an Eagles' cap and a gray ponytail who thinks these are the funniest damn jokes about BP's oil spill he's ever heard.

Above the bar, on the ceiling, are stately, dark wood beams that give the Inn a cottage-like feel. There's also a large Eagles blanket on the wall, and a stuffed animal grab game in the back, for some reason. In the restroom is a hand painted screeching Eagles' head logo, which was done either by a very talented nine-year-old or an adult with none-too-impressive motor skills. Beer is cheap. Pints of Bud are $1.75. It tastes a bit skunky, but at that price no one's complaining.

In the meantime, gray ponytail is chuckling to himself. The sound is turned way up on Leno, but the closed captioning is also on. Whoever's got the job of typing out Leno's jokes doesn't seem to find him as funny as this patch of drunks in the Northeast, as each joke he tells is followed with [Scattered applause]. The Celtics' tweaker, now in the bar, makes his way to where everyone is sitting, asking again if we were aware there was a cover charge tonight, laughing to himself. The bartender tells him to quit bothering people. She then gets her own bit of [Scattered applause].

Morrell Tavern

3800 Morrell Ave.
Phone: 215-632-6870

Dive Bar Rating

Outside the Morrell Tavern, another dive in the Great Northeast located in a strip mall, the fetid smell of trash is overwhelming. There are half a dozen or so dumpsters outside the bar's door, it's a hot day, and the sun has been baking the trash for hours. The smell is powerful, and can just about turn your insides out.

Inside Morrell, there's a hotly contested game of Texas Hold 'Em going on atop the pool table. The tournament has been going on all day, I'm told, and it's down to its last two players, both of whom have a similar size stack of chips. One of the players looses a big hand to the other, and keeps disappointingly calling himself a knucklehead as a result. The dealer wears a visor for ultimate authenticity.

Morrell doesn't have much in the way of variety beer-wise, just your typical big domestics. But what it lacks in choice of brand, it more than makes up for in choice of size, as they sell everything from seven ounce pony bottles for those planning a dainty night to 40 ounce bottles of hooch for those wanting to keep it strictly sloppy. Loads of pool trophies line the walls, displayed next to a couple Flyers' and Phillies' jerseys that are incased in glass. There's a hockey table game located under a sign that seems redundant at any bar: "No outside beverages allowed!" There's also a Guitar Hero set up in the back of the bar, but no one gives it much use. That could be due in part to the eardrum pounding intensity of the jukebox, which contains every Stone Temple Pilots song ever recorded and a clientele happy to give their catalogue a spin. Every so often a new customer walks in, and the faint whiff of the trash follows them in. A guy by the front door asks his friend if he's been using the loud music as audio camouflage for a torrent of farts he's been unleashing. He's quickly reminded of the rules of stealth crop dusting: You smelt it, you dealt it. "No," the friend says, pointing to the dealer. "He dealt it," before both erupt into unabated laughter. Knuckleheads.

SmokeEaters Pub

7681 Frankford Ave.
Phone: 215-338-4188

What Tailhook Tavern is to military paraphernalia, SmokeEaters is to firefighter gear. There are antique fire extinguishers on the wall, as well as ladders, helmets, jackets, boots, axes and hoses. In fact, the place looks more like a fireman's museum than a bar. There are also big signs on the wall that read "No fire department cutbacks," "offenders need just sentences" and notices for fundraisers for the families of police officers killed in the line of duty (which happens with alarming frequency in Philly). Not surprisingly, the place is owned by a fireman, and many of its clientele are fireman and their families from local Engine 14, Ladder 15.

The place is gigantic, and the long, seemingly football field length bar serves beer from the Hook and Ladder brewing company as a specialty, though mostly it's big domestics like Bud and Miller that get pulled here, especially on Sundays when a pint of each will cost you a scant $2. The food is standard bar fare, everything from jalapeno poppers to wings and mozzarella sticks. There's a full menu available for your perusal at smokeeaterspub.com, the look of which proves the old adage, "Firefighters make lousy graphic designers."

On the night I was here, things were relatively slow. There were no firemen as far as I could tell, but there was a very elderly woman sipping suds who had trouble keeping her head up and occasionally said things out loud to no one in particular. The bartender checked up on her frequently to see if she was okay, in the way an EMT might administer to someone who's just fallen off a motorcycle. "Ma'am. Ma'am. You doin' all right? Ma'am?" Come to think of it, at SmokeEaters, the bartender might be EMT certified.

Tailhook Tavern

Dive Bar Rating

3522 Cottman Ave.
Phone: 215-338-4027

There are just gobs and gobs of things to look at on the walls of the Tailhook Tavern, a tiny military bar located in a strip center in the Great Northeast. There are pencil sketches of Marine Rangers; a poster of former (allegedly racist) Mayor Frank Rizzo informing you he "means business"; a photo of John Wayne decked out in Army threads; and an airplane propeller, signed by the 49th Marine Air Logistics Squadron and given to Tailhook Owner Tom Devine upon his retirement.

And then there are patches, literally hundreds of them: Marine patches from different units, police patches from different districts, fireman patches, patches from the Philly bomb disposal unit, a patch from Vietnam Engine 5 Philly (The Big Nickel), even a patch for the canine rescue unit that worked the Twin Towers on 9/11. Along with the patches are tons of stickers, many of which make for good reading. "Do draft dodgers have reunions? If so, what do they talk about?" "We're Marines. We took Iwo Jima. Baghdad ain't shit!" But mostly what catches your eye at Tailhook is the honest to god real deal rocket launcher behind the bar. You *do not* want to walk out on your tab here.

Not that Tom's sister, Marie, here at the bar they own together, would harm a fly. She sees me eyeing the patches, and brings me a tiny Styrofoam plate of Bugles, the tastier-than-I-remember corn chip snack I didn't realize still existed. (And, by the way, Bugles being the snack of choice at a military bar—nice touch!) Tom was in the military for thirty-four years, and they opened the bar together when he retired seven years ago. She tells me there are more patches to look at in back, in the room with the pool table. And, yes, she knows John Wayne wasn't in the military, but he gets a pass. "He's *John Wayne*," she says in a way that suggests she didn't need to say it at all. "Come on!" She asks if my drink is okay. I ordered a whiskey soda. She made me a Seven and Seven. "It's great, thanks." (It actually is.) At the end of the bar sit two old vets, both nursing Budweisers and adjusting their hearing aids. They really complete the look of the place. I smile at them, and they smile back. God Bless America.

PHILADELPHIA'S TEN BEST DIVE BARS

Ray's Happy Birthday Bar

Friendly Lounge

Jack's Famous Bar

McGlinchey's

Dolphin Tavern

Bob & Barbara's

Jerry's Bar

Krupa's Tavern

Dirty Frank's

Oscar's Tavern

OTHER DIVES OF INTEREST

Al's Katnip Café, 412 S. 54th St. (West)

Connie's Ric Rac,

Riley's Lounge, 501 N. 52nd St. (West)

Paddy's Well, 1873 Frankford Ave. (North)

Scanlon's Saloon, 4201 Manayunk Ave. (Manayunk)

Fountain St. Pub, 343 Fountain St. (Manayunk)

Brick House Bar and Grill, 326 Roxborough (Roxborough)

Prince Café, 6732 Bustleton Ave. (Great Northeast)

Byrne's Tavern, 3301 Richmond St.

JW's Jack of Heart, 4105 Lancaster (West)

Swank Lounge, 60th and Chestnut sts. (West)

Edmondson's Lounge, 6004 Market St. (West)

Johnny Bear's, 1512 Lounge 112 W. Shunk (South)

Manny & Phil's Pub, 1801 S. 4th St. (South)

Handlebar, 1102 Frankford Ave. (North)

Cannonball Tavern, 2268 Kennedy St. (North)

Tadpole's Hole, 2014 Ridge Ave. (Set of Judgement Night)

The Pit, 39th and Walnut sts. (Secret after hours spot!) (West)

The Republican, 1734 Snyder Ave. (After hours strip club.) (South)

T Hogan's Pub, 1509 Rochelle Ave. (Manayunk)

Pernitsky's Bar, 401 N. George St. (North)

CENTER CITY DIVE CRAWL

This may very well be the most tightly packed collection of top-notch dives in the country. By the time you're done with all of these you'll have walked no more than fifteen blocks. And by walked I mean stumbled.

Oscar's Tavern > McGlinchey's > Pen & Pencil > Locust Rendez-vous > Locust Bar > Dirty Frank's > Bob & Barbara's > Tritone

WEST PHILLY DIVE CRAWL

There are two different dive crawls you can do pretty easily by foot or bike in West Philly. The first will take you up West Philly's "Main Street," 52nd Street:

Hide-A-Way Inn > Blue Nile Falls > Billie's Boomer Lounge > Smitty's Millcreek Tavern

The second will take you up Lancaster with a side jaunt to Belmont and Haverford:

BJ Lounge > New Angle Lounge > Way's Lounge > El Toro > Melody Lounge

NORTHERN LIBERTIES DIVE CRAWL

Not so much a crawl, since there are only really two of them, but they're both so fantastic, they're worth heading to anyway. For bonus points, hop on the El train at the Spring Garden station a short walk away, take it to the Allegheny stop, and go to Jack's Famous Bar.

Jerry's Bar > R.U.B.A. Hall > Spring Garden El station > Allegheny El station > Jack's Famous Bar

FISHTOWN DIVE CRAWL

Club Ozz > Fishtown Tavern > Fishtown's 15th Round > Gil's Goodtime Tavern > Luke's Bar > Tailgators (for one game of Maverick pinball, then leave) > Yesterday's Tavern

SOUTH PHILLY DIVE CRAWL

Cookie's Tavern > Rosewood Bar > Brothers II > DiNic's > Bonnie's Capistrano > Dolphin Tavern > Big Charlie's Saloon

GHOSTS OF DIVE BARS PAST

Wander Inn, 1800 Federal

La Creole Restaurant, 775 S. Front St.

Artful Dodger, 400 S. 2nd St.

McCusker's Tavern, 2601 S. 17th St.

Casbar, 56th and Spruce St.

The Cove, 3182 Richmond St.

Flynn's Bar, 40th and Market (Strangely, the lights are always on.)

Midtown IV, 2013 Chestnut St.

INDEX